What readers are saying about Echoes of the Heart!

"From the initial shock, through the litany of amazing stories, to the inspiring closing poems of yours, this is one powerful and empowering book. Admittedly, it's a lot to take in, but yet I strongly suspect it would help people of similar circumstances get some needed answers and help them heal their heart."

Jim Young – Award Winning Spiritual Author and Inspirational Speaker

"*Echoes of the Heart* is compelling, and also, educational. It shines light on a subject that needs to be better understood, as suicide is now the third leading killer of our youth."

Tolly Burkan – Founder of the Firewalking Movement

"From the very beginning this story has everything to keep you turning the page. The oddest thing is that it's true. I thought that I'd experienced difficulties in my life, but they're nothing compared to what happened to Caara as a result of the tragic death of her youngest son. I'm honored and blessed to have been a part of telling your story, Caara. You inspire me greatly."

Jim Rogers - Author, Holistic Life Counselor

Echoes of the Heart

The Power of Love
to Triumph over Tragedy

By
Caara Chantrel

For Christopher... and Karen

Acknowledgments

This book has been a *long* journey.

I could not have made this journey without the encouragement and help of Larry Cohn, Andrea Ward, Judith Cassis, Amy Abrams, Jim Rogers, Camille Nighthorse, Frank Aoi, my daughter Shelby, granddaughter Naomi, and others who breathed life into me, loved me, and reminded me to never give up.

A special thanks to each of you.

❦

May you walk softly through the journey of the heart —

Ciara   480-313-1690

Introduction

The road of life is one that has many blind corners, some of which we never see until.... It's the moments right after we encounter such blind corners that have great power to permanently shape our lives in ways that we never could have imagined, just seconds earlier.

Many times it's the trip around such a blind corner that reveals a route that we don't want to take, but to go on with life, we must.

This is the story of one person who had such an experience. Coming upon one of life's blind corners, an event took place which led the author to a life path that she knew she must take. What this route revealed to her was a new, different, and better person within her. It's also what this book is about.

Few people experience such an unspeakable trauma as Caara Chantrel. Yet as a result of this circuitous journey of healing, she's been transformed into a different person; an unstoppable force.

The story of Caara Chantrel is a compelling one that will inspire and educate you in ways that you would have never thought one's life story could.

One

In An Instant

All that I believed to be true, suddenly and painfully ended one day... the day that my precious 17-year-old son, Christopher, took his life. It's oft been said, *"What a difference a day makes,"* but even a second can make a difference. While I don't believe that his act was premeditated, in a moment of what seemed to be acute, spur-of-the-moment desperation, he placed the barrel of a gun to his head and... this is so hard to write... pulled the trigger.

Just yards away, I was close enough to hear the shot that will ring in my head forever, yet I was as powerless to stop him as if I were in another city, with my hands tied behind my back. Did he hear me pleading with him in those final moments? While I really can't be sure, if he did, it certainly didn't stop him from taking action.

Life is a circle—a series of beginnings and endings. Without warning, some doors slam shut, yet miraculously, others open ajar. Windows wedged shut can be pried and shimmied to once again rise. Fresh air blows in; light shines. This story, my story, paradoxically begins with an end... the closing of just such a window or door.

Questions of destiny readily follow disaster. Did Christopher choose death, or did death choose him? Either way, it was the most horrifying moment of my life.

Philosophers, families, and the forlorn have often pondered the mysteries of human existence since our dawn. I would come to understand that this single unbearable event would soon echo miracles, and gratitude would fill the hearts of many I would never come to know. Yet, in a stroke of providence, a very special woman would rise from the ashes of this devastation to be an agent of change and transformation for my broken life.

In the time that we'll spend together within these pages, I'll share my story with you. Not only is it a story of the heart, but a story of how love can hurt as much as it can also heal and create joy. This is a story that I'm compelled to share, and now, years later, perhaps many more lives will be helped, possibly even saved, through the publishing of this book. If but one life is changed through the sharing of my story, then I have fulfilled my mission.

I pray that my words will help anyone who's in pain, whether you, my reader, are someone who is or not.

Perhaps, like me, you're a mother who has been struggling to come to terms with your child's death or suicide, or maybe you're close to someone who's been doing their best to deal with this now. It could even be that you've contemplated taking your own life. You could also be someone who's donated or received an organ. Whoever you are, whatever your story, even if you're reading this book out of curiosity, I hope you'll take away something that makes your life better in some way.

Most of all, I hope, dear reader, that my words bring you peace. Whether you've experienced tragedy, or know someone else who has, my intention is that sharing my personal journey will, at the very least, offer you hope. Perhaps it will provide some meaning to a loss so horrific that no parent should ever have to experience. Extending my heart to you by writing this book has aided in my own healing; has helped me to continue taking steps across the threshold, through the doorway, and back to love.

I don't think that we'll ever fully understand those thoughts and feelings that motivate a person to take his or her own life. While it goes against the very laws of nature, it happens every day. For every successful attempt, it's estimated that eleven unsuccessful attempted suicides occur and these numbers continue to increase.

Although I know the circumstances surrounding my son's suicide, I'll never really know what caused him to cross the bridge between the will to survive and the desire to die. I'll never even know if he truly wished to end his life, or whether a fleeting, frivolous thought caused him to pull the trigger. I'll never know because I cannot ask him.

The gun can be a very final and unforgiving weapon, and ironically, its purposes are broad. It's an implement that's been used to feed the hungry, protect a family from danger, and in Christopher's case, to end a life that had barely begun.

There is always a desire to know the reasons behind a suicide and I've always wondered, as well. Was it Christopher's mission, or some random event in a planetary theatrical production that's beyond any human comprehension? No matter what, I know only one thing for sure, that in the wake of his death, Christopher saved the lives of several human beings. His broken body was salvaged and parts of him live on in the bodies of those who received his precious gifts.

Have you walked this road? If not, you may know someone who has. Yet no matter what, I ask you to open your heart to compassion – first for yourself, and then for any parent or family member who has suffered this unfathomable loss.

Echoes of the Heart chronicles the strength and power of love to endure in the face of complete and utter tragedy. It's the *story of the heart.*

And so we begin our journey, you and I...

To live in hearts we leave behind is not to die –

~ Thomas Campbell

Two

Awakening Into a Life Beyond Words

I awakened, unable to move. While at first I thought I'd just had a bad dream, the gnawing ache in my bones, and the heaviness in my heart, told me it was something much more than that. It wasn't long before my memory slowly began to reconstruct the confusing moments of the night before. A thousand thoughts crowded into my head from the fog that seemed to surround me. I wasn't even sure if what I recalled was real, yet suddenly the distant sound of a gunshot began to get louder and louder as it now began to reverberate within my head.

Slowly, grief swelled and the hole in my soul grew deep and dark.

And then I knew... It was true. My Christopher was *dead.*

My mouth opened to release a cry that rose from the

center of the earth... a cry from the heart of our terrestrial mother, mingled with the pain of all of the mothers who'd lost children through the ages. My body shook with sobs as this reality hit me like an earthquake.

Then I felt it... *the beat of Christopher's heart.*

I pushed aside the sheets and struggled out of bed, still drugged by the medication the doctor had given me to "soften the pain." *Soften the pain?* There's *no medication available* (legal or illegal) that's strong enough to relieve this pain! Yet even so, the meds, coupled with sheer exhaustion, had somehow helped me sleep.

I was so numb as I blankly searched through my purse for the card that the transplant team had given me. The night before, I'd left the hospital as soon as they told me that Christopher was "brain dead," yet I was also keenly aware that Christopher's spirit had already left his body. I had no doubt whatsoever. In fact, I knew it the moment that I'd heard the gunshot.

Later, I would wonder why I'd left the hospital (but since then I've learned not to question behavior when in the midst of a traumatic situation). In spite of the blurred haze I was in, I was somehow comforted in recalling that my older son, Brian, had remained with Christopher's body until the harvest team had completed their work.

"Organ harvesting" refers to the practice of removing usable organs from a designated donor who is declared by a physician to be "brain dead," so that the organs can be transplanted into someone else. In order for an organ to be donated, it's often required that some kind of brain injury be present while vital parts of the body remain intact. During the "preparation phase," the body must be held on life support while "donor status" is officially determined.

Every day in hospitals and homes across the globe, people die while waiting for the transplant of a vital organ, whether that be a heart, liver, kidney, pancreas, lung, or bone marrow. The loving act of tissue donation from a single donor can enhance the lives of more than fifty people.

Of course, organ donation is *only* considered after it is determined that a patient has no hope of survival. A preliminary team arrives first, before the harvest team. Consisting of one or two people, they talk with the family about the possibility of donating organs or other viable tissues. The wishes of surviving family members are always respected and even in the most dire of circumstances, organ harvesting never takes place without consent.

Compounded by shock and grief, organ donation can be a difficult choice for many to make. However the clock continues to tick and decisions must often be made quickly, as was the case in Christopher's situation. An organ must be transplanted within a few hours for the operation to be successful. Time was of the essence, so grief and pain would have to wait. I tried to think clearly and make the most loving choices as I did my best to hold back the shock of my son's sudden and tragic exit from this life.

Three

The Gift

Somewhere in the midst of the vast dark void of that winter night, someone must have heard the gunshot and called 911. The police arrived soon after Christopher shot himself. They ushered me back to my son's car where I sat alone and in shock, as if frozen in time.

Later, when I asked the police why they'd just left me there, I was told that, no matter what, the site of a suicide is always treated as a crime scene. It's just that in the business of examining their crime scene, they had unintentionally forgotten about me. Afterward there would be a sincere apology, as well as an explanation to allay any misgivings. But the mystery, or as it turned out, *the gift* that I was offered in being left alone would soon reveal itself.

There I sat, in Christopher's Geo Tracker... *alone*. Three hours had passed since Christopher had ended his life with a bullet. I'd noted the time of the gunshot, as I knew in my heart the very moment that Christopher's spirit was gone-- near the stroke of midnight. I didn't note the time again until I walked into the hospital and there in the intensive care room was a clock that read 3:00 a.m. *Three hours* had passed... hard to believe in light of what would come next.

Encased within the bellowing blast of the gun, and the reality of my son's death that was slowly descending into my consciousness, these seemingly altered moments passed as though they were raindrops eternally lost atop a vast ocean. As I sat there in Christopher's car, I was about to experience the first of several miracles.

Although it *appeared* there was no one with me, I hadn't really been alone in the Geo Tracker. Suddenly in the silence, I became aware of a sacred presence. Gently, peacefully, I was bathed in a warm pink glow that wrapped itself around me like a silken cocoon. Later, as I reflected on this, it felt to me that this nurturing presence was the love of Mother Mary, who in the depth of her compassion drew me close to her heart. I felt as though I was sitting at the foot of the cross with the broken body of my son, returning him from whence he came. As I sat there in shock, this soft, warm glow held me in my grief.

From the midst of this silent void came a message that I heard and understood with my heart.

On an intellectual level, the best way I can describe my experience is to say that during the stillness of these moments, I received an infusion of information from a sacred presence that spoke with no words. Yet my brain tracked every element of the message, complete with details of what to do and how it should be done... a direction to donate Christopher's organs.

Organ donation... I had never known any family member to be a donor, and I can say that in light of the tragic situation into which I was now thrust, I may never even have thought of it on my own. But over time, as bits and pieces of memories became clear, I reflected on a conversation that Christopher and I had once had about organ donation. Had it been a foreshadowing of what lie in wait for my son?

During the twelve months before his death, Christopher had experienced many rites of passage in his young life. He had only recently gotten his driver's license. When he returned home after the exam, he was so excited that he'd passed.

"Let me see your picture," I said.

Christopher reached into his wallet and handed me his license. On the donor space was a sticker that read, *No.*

I was curious, so I asked, "Why did you answer *'no' under organ donation?"*

He looked at me and said, "I want all my parts, Momma".

I laughed and said, "We will discuss it and I know you'll want to change it."

Christopher smiled and said, "Okay".

There had been many times, after hearing an explanation of my thoughts concerning a particular subject, that Christopher would change his mind to be in agreement with me. I knew this kindhearted son of mine well enough to know that once he understood, he would be glad to give the gift of life to someone else, as he was a true believer in always helping those who were somehow less fortunate.

Christopher had once made a tape for a school project about appreciation. He talked of his appreciation for his brother Brian, his father, Richard, and me. He appreciated that even though his brother Brian had experienced a hard life as an addict, he had remained a kind and good brother. Mentioning his father, Christopher spoke about Richard's strength and kindness as a man. He also spoke of how he appreciated each of his organs. He named his liver, his heart, and his lungs, mentioning how each of them had served him. When he came to me, he said if he had to use one word to describe his mom, it would be "magical" ... that I "could take any problem, turn it around, and with words make it... okay."

Not this time, son.

Tears rolled down my face as I wondered... *'Why didn't my yelling for you to not shoot yourself stop you?'*

The eternal cries of humankind's suffering rose within me from my gut, and then dropped me to my knees.

Why Christopher?

Why me?

How could this have happened?

I wanted him back with a desperate yearning. No parent should be put in a position to contemplate such choices. Yet, somehow, I could perceive... through the blackest of nights... the light.

Now in the moments following Christopher's death, held in the softness of the shimmering pink glow, I received these instructions for my next steps. I had no prior knowledge of the specific requirements that needed to be met for a body to be considered for organ donation. While I knew that his spirit was gone, I knew nothing about the actual state of Christopher's physical body. In order for a donor to be a candidate, the body must be living long enough to be placed on life support, until pronounced brain dead.

For all I knew, Christopher's body had died the moment he shot himself, the moment I had felt his spirit leave. Still, I listened and took in the information. It was as though my mind was cleared of all thinking and my brain was an empty vessel, now receiving information.

During those quiet moments in the car I have absolutely no doubt that I was being divinely led. I sat in silence for three hours, not asking one question and not really being told anything by the police. Nevertheless, I clearly knew what needed to be done. Using contemporary language, you might say the information was *downloaded* into my mind in the same way information is downloaded into a computer. I look back now and marvel at how this happened.

The next few hours were surreal. I believe they were among the most difficult that any parent could be forced to survive. And yet life, as part of its divine process, gave me what I needed to pull through this, as I was about to hear the words that no one wants to hear when it concerns the life of a loved one.

· Four ·
Wait For Me
at Heaven's Door

Their work complete at the "crime scene," the police finally took me to the hospital. As we entered the Emergency Room at the lower level of the building, a lovely lady met me. She told me that she was a volunteer crisis manager and that she was there to assist me. Her face was kind, and her voice gentle, as she delivered what had to be difficult words.

With compassion filling her eyes, she said, "I want you to know before I take you upstairs, there is no hope." Once these words were spoken, she gently lowered her gaze.

Those words... *There is no hope.*

I replied, "I know."

Following the instructions I had been given by the sacred presence earlier, I said, "Please call the transplant agency and tell them that I want to donate any organs possible."

Normally, the transplant team would show up once they were contacted by the hospital, informing them there was a possible donor. They would then contact the closest relative and ask for permission to harvest any viable organs. Yet I had already received the echo of the heart, so I simply requested the team.

The woman accompanied me to Christopher's room in the ICU, where I saw him lying in the bed, his head wrapped with layers of blood-soaked gauze. He was connected to a breathing machine. He looked alive, just asleep. Although he looked much the same as the many times I'd gazed at his sleeping face, from the time he was a baby, I knew without question that here and now there was something very different.

Yes, for me his spirit was gone... in another time and place.

My chest felt hollow. My mind tried to deny what I knew to be true. I folded down the covers on his 17-year-old body just as I had when he was a newborn baby. I rubbed my hands over his hands and feet and bathed his face in my tears and told him over and over how much I loved him.

As I caressed my son, a flood of memories came and went. I realized that my duty now had changed from that of being his mother, teacher, nurturer and more, to preparing his body for leaving this earth. I asked the head nurse to call a Bishop from the Mormon Church. My Bishop was out of town, so a young Bishop from another ward came in his place. He anointed Christopher's head with consecrated oil and gave him a beautiful blessing to leave this earth. I felt the heavens open and the veil became thin, as the young Bishop performed a sacred ordinance. I cannot remember his name but will forever be thankful that he heard the call... and came.

Another remembrance surfaced... of a time when Christopher was brought to his father and me, at age three, in the Seattle Temple. Dressed in his little white suit, he was sealed to us for all time and eternity, a holy seal that now gave me comfort in my time of need. My mind lingered briefly with this memory before I came back to the reality of preparing for the journey of the heart.

As I was already committed to "donating," it wasn't long before the transplant team arrived and the moment came for planning new journeys for the organs that Christopher had once *appreciated*. Instead of asking me if I'd be willing to donate organs, the team would quickly begin to learn from the medical staff which organs remained viable. I was asked to answer questions about the history of Christopher's health, how long he'd had his tattoos and what blood type he was--all of the things that a mother would know. Christopher's tattoo was barely a month old, and for this reason, sadly his corneas couldn't be considered for donation. Was this tattoo upon his chest yet another foretelling? The words read, "do or die."

The process moved along rather quickly. Once all the paperwork was complete, I signed the documents that would allow the transplant team to do all of the necessary procedures on Christopher's body in order to save the lives of several recipients.

Simultaneously, the nursing staff began the flushes and processes required to prepare the body for organ harvesting once the donor is pronounced brain-dead. I learned that people of all ages qualify, both to donate and receive healthy transplant organs. Time was rushing forward and the team was doing all it could to prepare for the harvest of all that was viable from Christopher's body.

After Christopher was officially pronounced brain-dead, a nurse came in and told me the harvest team had arrived. The sound of those words always will always ring in my head... *harvest team.* It's one thing to contemplate, and yet another to take action. I was blessed by my experience in Christopher's car earlier that night which allowed me to ease into a decision that is so difficult for so many. Due to deep emotional pain coupled with time constraints, many family members are unable to even consider such an option. Yet, I have such gratitude that I didn't have to face that struggle. Even in the midst of my numbness I knew there was a blessing... in the knowing.

Yes, this was really happening. Unlike the welcoming moment of birth, this was the moment when death calls for the final goodbye. I whispered to Christopher, "Honey, wait for me at Heaven's Door".

Kissing him goodbye, I turned and walked out of the room, unable to look back.

It was the hardest thing that I've ever done....

Five

Time for the Harvest

The *harvest team* - What did they do and how did they do it? As I began to live life without Christopher, I wondered about this and revisited the scene often in my mind. While somewhere down the road answers would come, for a long time, I was left only to wonder.

My romantic partner of five years, Ross, had been concerned for my well-being. At his insistence I had left the hospital once the harvest team had arrived, so I could barely even begin to speculate about the process. If I could relive that night once again I would do things differently. First of all, I would have either stayed or at least I would have made plans to go home and rest then come back. Hindsight: friend or foe?

Many times over, I wished that I would've lingered a while longer with Christopher's lifeless body. I've also wished that I would have inquired about the harvest process, as I had no idea whether the harvest team would leave the body in a state that would allow for an open casket. Since that time, I've been told by the nurses who'd served on the harvest team that they refill the cavity of the body so that it appears to be intact. While the medical staff of the harvest team must work quickly to keep organs usable, they also remain respectful of the donor. Once the procedure is finished they ensure that the patient is sewn up so that the family, if they desire, can visit the body as part of their grieving process.

Nevertheless, I will always be grateful for the eight hours that I was given to say my goodbyes to Christopher's physical body. I left trusting that the harvest team would take what they could use. My heart knew that many lives would be assisted by this tragic loss.

I awakened the next morning to one booming command demanding an answer.

Who had Christopher's heart?

I needed to know. With trembling fingers, I dialed the number of the transplant agency. The lady who answered my call said that the person who'd handled transplantation had not yet completed recording the details. She promised to contact me as soon as she could gather the information.

And so... I waited.

In my reflection, I could feel the beat of Christopher's love filling the emptiness within my soul. I could *feel him* calling out to me, and thus it became critical for me to know how his heart was doing. I find it fascinating that I never felt curious about the recipients of his other organs. Yet I knew, without a doubt, that Christopher's heart was calling out to me.

A mother knows.

· Six ·

In Search
of the Heart

That first day passed as if in slow motion. Several hours after I'd made my initial call to the transplant agency, the phone finally rang. Hurriedly grabbing it on the first ring, I was relieved to hear the voice of a man on the other end of the line. He was calling with information about Christopher's organ harvest, and I was so anxious to speak with him.

First of all, he delivered some disappointing news as he explained that they were unable to use Christopher's lungs due to transport logistics. There simply hadn't been enough time to transport them to a recipient. It's sad to think that someone might have been out there in need of a lung transplant and because of time, distance, or whatever other variables, a perfectly good pair of lungs could not be gifted.

However, this man also had good news for me. A football coach in Tucson had received Christopher's liver. *How amazing. Christopher so loved football.* He would have been happy to know that his liver went to a kindred spirit. The recipient was a man who loved kids and had helped start a school that was named after him... a school for kids who had problems. Yet there was more good news as he went on to tell me that they had also harvested skin, bones, tissue and the pancreas, adding that some of the organs would be used for scientific research. My granddaughter, Misty, had been diagnosed at the age of ten with childhood diabetes because of a bad pancreas, so I was particularly pleased that his pancreas would be used to study this disease.

And what of the heart? I waited to hear...

He continued by telling me that they'd almost lost Christopher's heart because the kidneys had shut down due to shock as a result of the gunshot wound. However, they were ultimately able to save it and a 49-year-old woman with a 12-year-old son was blessed to be its recipient.

I closed my eyes and intuitively went deep within... to the depths of my being.

In my heart, I could feel her... there was no doubt in my being... and now I wanted to know more about her. *Who was she? Where did she live?* So far, the information was limited, and all this man could tell me was that this woman worked in the medical industry. However, to protect her privacy, they couldn't tell me her name. Out of my own need to contact her, I decided to give her a name. I named her

Brave Heart. Yet, what I didn't know was that *Brave Heart* was also seeking me.

Not far away in a Tucson hospital, a woman named Karen lay recovering after receiving Christopher's heart. Following an agonizing two-year wait, she'd finally received notification by her beeper, a steadily pulsing sound, just like the rhythmic beat of the heart that would save her life. Karen's heart had been fast failing and unresponsive to a host of therapies. Once added to the recipient list by her medical team, she also got beepers for her 12-year-old son, Justin, and fiancé, Russ, for emergency contact in hopeful preparation.

A heart donor and recipient are matched by both blood type and similar body weight. Once a match has been made, the donor heart must be transplanted no more than six hours after it's been harvested. Karen had already received a call for a heart once before, but was visiting Canada when it came and could not return to Arizona in time to receive it. The chances of receiving another call for a donor heart within range are often very slim. However, Karen lived in Scottsdale, just 20 minutes from me, and was at home this time when her beeper went off.

At any given moment around the globe, over 5,000 patients are waiting for a heart. Getting a match is likened to winning the lottery... and better than money, even millions... this is the priceless opportunity to continue one's life.

Upon hearing her beeper, Karen first paged her fiancé, only to hear a sickening sound, that of his own pager ringing in her kitchen. That morning, amid an especially harried "morning rush," he'd absent-mindedly abandoned it on the counter and was on the road. In the tough-to-recall age before cell phones, she now wondered how she would make the two-hour drive to Tucson on a notoriously congested highway. With her thoughts beginning to race, she thought of her son who had also somehow forgotten to take his pager with him that day. This was beginning to feel like an unusual set of either ill-starred or ill-fated circumstances, yet Karen had scant energy for contemplating anything other than getting to the heart. The seconds continued to tick by as she remembered the words of her doctor... that it's imperative to get to the hospital within three hours. Hardly able to walk, and severely short of breath, she hoisted herself out of the living room recliner to take some form of action.

Now that this moment had finally arrived, she found herself wholly unprepared. For quite some time she'd been meaning to pack the little suitcase for her hospital stay, and set it by the front door, yet she'd still done nothing. Was it a defense mechanism against holding too much hope that had prevented her from completing such a small act of faith...

or, perhaps, was it fear? Years later, when Karen and I had became as close as sisters, we often shared either sad or unexpectedly humorous anecdotes of the journey of the heart. Once she told me amid laughter, "Well, I recall thinking if I die, I won't need any clothes and if I live, I want all new clothes." Humor, and a really witty sense of humor at that, is what got both Karen and me through a lot over the years.

In a state of unbridled enthusiasm, and propelled by a hefty dose of panic, Karen grabbed nothing but her purse and crumpled into the front seat of her 1984 Lincoln. Starting it, then backing out of the garage into the light of the day, she was determined to make her way toward hope. While she always felt that this car had style and spunk, and she loved her big boat, it was not about to cooperate with her plans to take it, and her, to Tucson. Soon it began to sputter, and then stopped and lurched, as she barely coaxed it into a Denny's parking lot.

Polite to the core, Karen chose not to interrupt, but instead patiently waited for an elderly gentleman to complete his call on the pay phone nearby. Once the phone was available, which seemed like an eternity to her as the seconds continued to tick by, she rang and reached her doctor, who sternly commanded that she drive straight to Paradise Valley Hospital, just blocks away, where a helicopter would be waiting to fly her to Tucson.

With a bit more coaxing, the Lincoln made it the final few blocks to the hospital where Karen was whisked away to the awaiting chopper. Now safely strapped into the gurney, beneath raging motors and whirling blades, Karen lifted off, briefly hovered, and finally began flying toward the hospital in Tucson and her new life-giving heart.

Unlike an airplane, a helicopter takes flight by forces working in opposition to each other, which strikes me as a metaphor for both the tragic and glorious events of that January day. Karen recalls sensing at this great height, where angels and faeries are said to fly, that this offering came not only for her, but also for her son, so she might usher him through high school and, hopefully, even college, as well.

Upon landing in Tucson, she was hurriedly wheeled into the O.R. where an anesthesiologist prepared her to "go under." Years later, Karen shared that she was surprisingly unaware that she would be "heartless" for several hours while she was connected to machines that would sustain her.

Almost simultaneously, Christopher's heart was extracted from his lifeless body, wrapped in varied protectants, placed in a picnic cooler, and flown to Tucson on this emergent rescue mission.

In the years since this happened, I've read studies that show it is common for surgery patients to recall various, or spurious, aspects of their operation, and Karen recalls hearing the nurses and doctors conversing back and forth with one another. The phenomenon is known as "Anesthesia Awareness," and she remembers hearing the doctor asking the nurse for a body parts bag. While she didn't have one, he said, "it doesn't matter, the heart is so damaged that we will just trash it." Karen loved the heart that had served her and she thought that she would be able to bury it or honor it in some way. Upon awakening and slowly coming to, she also remembers her first thought. Her initial words, whispered to her son and fiancé, as Christopher's heart infused her with a new "life-force" were, "Find me the mother of the heart."

Her family members did their best to locate me, scouring the Scottsdale paper, yet found no news of an accident claiming the life of a 17-year-old male. Ironically, the information they sought had been printed in the paper of the neighboring city of Phoenix.

Later when Karen described these moments to me, she said, "All I wanted was *you* by my side".

"Yes, I know", I told her.

The *heart called out* in every way that it could. I knew this with a mother's knowing, that intuitive process that surpasses understanding and alerts her when her child is in trouble. I could feel it in my soul. I had never doubted hearing the echo of his heart, even in the midst of my pain.

Seven

The Ashes Come Home

The days following Christopher's death were long and agonizing. The process was an excruciating one that was consumed with planning his memorial service and making several difficult decisions. Among these were the choices of either burial or cremation. Yet, amid my loss, I held onto the belief that God is kind. He sheltered me with a numbness that held my ripped soul as I made decisions no parent ever expects to make... decisions for their child's final rest. Although some family members had strong opinions to the contrary, I finally decided upon cremation.

Cremation often serves as an alternative to the interment of an intact body in a casket. Remains may be buried, placed at memorial sites, legally retained by loved ones, or dispersed in a variety of ways and locations.

In hindsight, I found myself wishing that I would have had an open casket viewing so the rest of the family and

Christopher's friends could gain their own closure. He'd just been with his friends on Friday night and the funeral was held the following Tuesday. In retrospect, I can now see that his peers approached the loss in a different manner. Without the myriad details I had painfully endured, step-by-step, to integrate the reality of this death, they were not yet confronted by the reality of his passing. In my own fog, I was unable to see how my decisions, made out of shock and grief, would affect the many others who also loved Christopher.

Once the process was complete, I prepared to bring Christopher home.

After cremation, if you don't have an urn in which to place them, the ashes come home in a cardboard box. So, I had picked out a beautiful handmade Myrtle wood urn for Christopher's ashes, a wood that's native to Oregon, Christopher's birthplace, and reputed as sacred wood due to its appearance in the Old Testament book of Isaiah. (The prophet Isaiah spoke of the tree saying, "Instead of the brier shall come up the Myrtle tree" Isaiah 55:13.)

I, too, was raised in Oregon—in the Oregon Mountains —and the fragrant scent of the tree's yellowish-white blossoms is still with me in memory.

It was for this very reason, a symbolic return home for Christopher, that Myrtle wood seemed to be ideal for this vessel. It is said that Myrtle wood only grows in the Holy Land and in Oregon. In the Bible, the Myrtle tree is of special religious significance, representing fertility and life. Although a larger tree with a little different flower type, Oregon Myrtle wood has a lot of similarities to the Myrtle tree that grows in the Holy Land.

The urn had been crafted by a Native American artist and had been beautifully decorated with inlaid turquoise. Since Christopher's great-great-grandmother (my great-grandmother) was Cherokee, he felt a deep connection to these roots and loved the fact that he had Native American blood running through his veins, and so do I. It was especially because of its Native American origin that this beautiful piece of artwork held such great spiritual meaning for me.

Eight days after Christopher's death, his ashes finally came home. The day was somber. I'd set up an altar with candles and created a beautiful space in which to welcome Christopher's ashes.

Eight

Balancing Many Hearts

Unlike many former spouses in the wake of a divorce, my ex-husband, Richard, and I had remained close friends. Three weeks following Christopher's death, Richard had quadruple bypass surgery, and since we were still friends, I went to spend ten days in Seattle caring for him. The hospital where he had surgery had an extensive library, which provided me with many hours of reading by Richard's bedside. From time to time, the chaplain would come by and sit with me and in these times when we would talk with one another, I shared with him about Christopher. After what I'd just experienced with my son, he couldn't believe that I was here sitting with a heart patient. I just responded, "Who better than me?"

Richard had known me since I was 12-years-old and we'd married when I was only the tender 14 years of age.

By the time I was 23, I had given birth to four children, two sons and two daughters.

Christopher was my baby, a late-in-life child who was born when I was all of 36. Each of my older children was now grown, with children and busy lives all their own. Scattered about and living in several different states, each of them would deal with Christopher's death in their own way.

When I divorced their father, Christopher was twelve. He and I had moved alone to Arizona where we began our lives again. We had now been apart from my other children for four years. Perhaps for the rest of the family, especially since I didn't have a viewing of the body at his service, it felt as if Christopher was still just away.

Yes, who better than me... one whose own heart had been torn out. I was also one who understood first-hand, a heart being given, a heart being received, and now, a heart being repaired. It appeared to be metaphorical to me... the circle of life.

For a long time after Christopher's death, I walked around with my hand on my own heart—my palm pressed firmly upon my chest for soothing and protection. I could feel such emptiness there. Conversations I've had with other mothers who had lost children reflected that they, too, felt the sensation of a hole in their chest. Occasionally, I've also met surviving siblings of those who've died at a young age. When I've asked how their mothers were doing, remarkably they expressed similar sentiments such as, "She feels like she has a hole in her chest. She feels like her soul has been torn apart."

Yes, I understood. Through sharing stories with others who had suffered the loss of a child, I began to comprehend that we all have the same conversations, that same empty space, and the same holes in our chests. We understand each other as only those who have sustained such a loss could. We know well that "missing" feeling.

• Nine •
Little Acts of Kindness

Time kept its relentless pace. Amidst my agony, in what seemed to be a mocking manner, the sun rose high in the beautiful sky each day. Then at sunset, tones of pink and lilac were splashed across the Arizona landscape. However, beauty could not yet find me in my grief. I would call the transplant agency every few days and ask, "How is the heart doing?" Each time I called they would always remind me that I would have to wait a year before making any attempt to contact the recipient.

I couldn't just *wait*. I needed to *do* something, so I began putting journals and picture albums together along with stories about Christopher. I did this for *Brave Heart...* because I wanted her to know my son, the person whose heart now beat inside her and gave her life. Knowing that the heart that I'd birthed still beat upon this Earth offered me some solace. Through the gathering and documenting and sharing, my own heart slowly began to heal.

In the midst of difficult times, the kindness of others means so much. We aren't always aware of what's going on in the life of another. We pass people on the street and have no idea what stories lie behind a blank stare or a conjured smile. Perhaps we've offered a gesture of kindness that's made a difference - even if for a moment. Often it means more than we'll ever come to know and it happens every day. It happened for me many times as I was piecing my life back together after Christopher's death. Once in particular, I recall the kindness from a stranger that lightened my load.

In the first few weeks after Christopher's passing, I had been working diligently to put together the albums for Brave Heart. In fact, I practically lived at Kinko's as I'd felt more than compelled to create the photo journals to send to the transplant agency. If anything, it almost felt like a calling. One day a clerk asked what I was doing.

"I'm creating albums for the woman who received my son's heart through transplantation."

I told her my story and she was obviously touched. When I went to pay for the copies, the clerk kindly said, "I talked to the manager. You may make as many photo journals as you wish and you don't have to pay for the copies."

Ahhhh... what the salve of kindness can do for an anxious, healing heart. *My heart* was in full production of the life story of the heart now sitting in the body of *Brave Heart.*

Once I had the finished creating each of the albums, I boxed and mailed them to the transplant agency. Upon receiving them, they would call and remind me they could not pass them on. Even though somehow I knew it didn't really matter, creating the albums was as much a healing therapy for me as it was a potential gift for *Brave Heart.* I was comforted to know that at some point in time, she would receive, read, and come to know the story of her heart.

Yet, complying with instruction, the employees at the transplant agency couldn't tell me each time I called that Brave Heart had also been calling them to ask, "Who is the mother of the heart?" She was given the same instruction, "It is suggested that a year needs to pass before contact is made."

I had once run a program called "Friends In Need," and had studied for several weeks with Elisabeth Kubler-Ross, who was the master teacher concerning how to deal with the dying. Many know of her by her groundbreaking bestseller, *On Death and Dying.* It was suggested in her work that after someone died, the family should wait a year before making any major changes. While I understood this line of reasoning, what seemed odd is that now I was seeking the "living." At this point in time a year seemed like an eternity to me, so I continued to follow the yearning of a mother's heart to hear the beat of her son's heart.

• Ten •

Fill Your Hearts With Courage and Love

The services for Christopher were now over and the flowers had begun to fade. I remember the day that the cards, the ones that had meant so much to me as they flowed in daily, stopped flowing. I missed the letters and encouraging notes that came in that first week after Christopher's death, and now I found myself going to the mailbox several times a day, just to check. Along with the vigilance of support that I gained from them in those first days, they also sustained me. If you've ever experienced the death of a loved one, I'm sure you can relate to those first few moments as you stand alone against the winds of life. Now that your friends and family have gone back to their own lives, you know that you have to go on even when everything inside of you just wants to lie down and go to sleep... forever.

I was left alone with my thoughts – the gnawing questions and the incessant wondering... *Why?*

I tore the house apart looking for signs... a note or *anything* that would offer even a hint as to why Christopher would take his life. Yet I found nothing... not a single clue that would lead me to believe that his suicide had been premeditated. There weren't even any hints that he was depressed enough to even contemplate such an ending. The truth is that even if I *had* found something, what reasoning would have been deemed *good enough* for him to have done such a thing? Nothing *would* ever, nor *could ever,* offer me peace of mind.

There was also nothing that could bring Christopher back. No recounting of details; the "what ifs," even when relived a thousand times over in my mind, would never bring me solace. My child was dead and that was all there was to it.

Christopher and I had left the house after a family argument, the kind that often happens between a teenage boy and an adult who is not his parent. We drove to the Comfort Inn where I secured a room for the night, hoping that things would blow over by morning. After registering and getting the key, I came back out to the car to get Christopher, and said, "Let's go in, son. Things will be better in the morning." He slowly got out of the car, reached into the back and pulled out his high school backpack. Reaching into his backpack, he pulled out a gun in a holster. The moment was surreal. My body went into full force shock.

Without warning, he began to run from me into the darkness, a darkness that held a full moon. I ran after him, and finally catching him, I tried my best to hold onto him.

I wanted to hold his young life and make everything okay, like any mother does... but I wasn't strong enough. He broke free of my grasp and ran into the night. I screamed for my son, desperate to locate him in the darkness, but was unable to catch up to him. It is interesting how, when one is in shock that you cannot see.

"Kill me, too," I remember screaming as I chased him into the dark night those last few minutes before the gunshot hung in the night air, "Please, Christopher—kill me, too!"

And he did. For that night, in the darkness the person I knew myself to be, died right there with him.

My heart grieved in the days and weeks following Christopher's death. The loss was unbearable. My body ached terribly. For relief, I would sometimes take six showers a day and just scream as the rushing water drowned out my wailing and washed away my tears. I felt like a mother wolf, wailing for her lost pup. Around that time, I found a story that Christopher had written. It was called, *The Christopher Holliday Story*, a story that had been written by Christopher two weeks before he died. Once several years had passed, its meaning would become clearer to me.

The Christopher Holliday Story

This is the story of a young man named Christopher,
His talking dog, Gray, and their journey into the spirit world.

Back in time unknown, there was a young man named Christopher and a dog named Gray. Gray was much more than a pet. He was Christopher's best friend, his companion.

On a day also unknown, Christopher and Gray sat high on a branch, atop an exotic tree. They were sharing their feelings and thoughts about life and love. Christopher talked about a love he once had for a beautiful girl. He spoke of how he'd lost this girl and her love because of his own greed and carelessness.

As Christopher told Gray his story, he explained that this event occurred in the time of the great black heart, before he met Gray. As Gray listened to Christopher, he was unaware that his mind had slowly drifted to another time and space in his own private world. Gray saw visions of his father teaching him different hunting skills and survival techniques. Tears began to fall from Gray's black eyes.

Christopher had been talking about his long, lost love when he noticed tears on his companion's face.

Christopher asked, "Why do you cry?"

Gray did not answer. Instead he cried more. Christopher sat close to Gray and tried to comfort him.

Gray continued mumbling and within a few minutes it was clear to Christopher that Gray was reminiscing about his father. Gray's father had been dead for a couple of years. He died of old age. He was a very wise old wolf, who had pretty much raised both Christopher and Gray.

Gray cleared the tears from his eyes, took some deep breaths and asked, "Do you think there really is a spirit world like my father said?"

Christopher said, "I don't know."

"My father said I could visit him there after he was dead and also visit the other spirits."

Christopher gazed at the sky and said, "There is a way, Gray, and we both know it."

"Your father said, 'Take your souls to a high peak, fill your hearts with courage and love, and if you truly believe there is a spirit world, you will jump from this peak and spread your arms like a bird and fly. If you truly believe - and if courage and love have filled your heart - a door will open in the air and suck you in.

I didn't know it at the time, but years later, Gray's identity was to be revealed to me in yet another cruel twist of fate.

The days passed and painful as it was for me to do, piece by piece, I began to sort through Christopher's things. Every sheet of paper held a meaning for me. I went through

Christopher's room, holding each piece of clothing as I picked it up, smelling it, remembering where we bought each item. We so enjoyed shopping together for clothes. I sprayed his cologne and could not believe how its scent held such memories of my child.

One day while I was in Seattle taking care of Richard, a friend called. While she was cleaning my house, she had gone through Chris's room and washed all of his clothes. I knew that she had meant well and was trying to do everything she could to make life easier for me, but I was devastated. I just sat down and cried. The main way that I had clung to Christopher's memory was by hanging onto the clothes that held his scent. Now that they'd been washed, they held less of his memory for me. In hindsight I realize that my friend was an angel unaware. Through her innocent act, she had provided a gentle forced nudge that helped me to begin letting go.

Life was reduced to a series of passages. Some days were better than others, and thanks to the support of my family, I was learning to cope. Yet nothing could prepare me for the phone call I would receive one day, out of the blue.

Eleven

Guns

One morning I received a call from the property division of the police department. The voice on the other end of the line said, "I am calling to tell you that you can pick up the property from the event on January 5."

I had to pause a moment to reflect on his words: "*the event?*"

I asked, "What do you have?"

He answered, "A backpack with Crayolas in it and a 9 millimeter gun with bullets."

For a moment, I stopped breathing.

The man went on to say that since six months had passed, and no one had claimed the gun, it was mine. I was suspended in time as I began to recall another time and place when a gun had pierced my soul. This call telling me that I could pick up the gun that my son had killed himself with triggered an old wound. In that moment, through the clouds, another memory began to take form....

I was 21-years old and pregnant with my third child, Shelby. I had just driven my 11-year-old brother to his friend's house and was headed back home, about a 30-minute drive. I'd just walked into the house when the phone rang. It was the sheriff's department, calling to tell me that my little brother had been killed by a gun. He'd been shot through the back.

Just 30 minutes before, he'd been in my car...

My brother and I were far enough apart in age that he was more like my son to me than anything else. How could he be dead? I had just left him at his friend's house to play.

My brother had been killed by another 11-year-old boy who got mad at him in a silly dispute about playing with a train. The boy went into his older brother's room, grabbed his 22 rifle and shot my brother through the back. Two boys had been playing and now, in a matter of 30 minutes one was dead. A gun is such an unforgiving weapon.

My brother was killed in 1963, the same year President Kennedy was shot by Lee Harvey Oswald. I had read many articles about gunshot wounds. I remember the questions: *Could the President have lived if he'd been shot in a different area of the brain?...*and on and on. I wondered the same thing about my brother. Could he have lived if the bullet went in an inch to the right or left? Questioning...*what if... if only*... another phase of the grieving process.

It wasn't enough that my brother had died. Out of sheer agony, my father had gone insane with grief and in a moment of anger, he shot a man and was then arrested for attempted murder. My father, who had been sober for some time, now began to drink away his grief following my brother's death. He never recovered, nor did my mother. She grieved herself to death from a broken heart at the age of 54.

I lost Christopher... at the age of 54.

I wondered: *Has the ready access to deadly weapons determined the destiny of my family? Has this trail of grief been imprinted into my soul?*

Yes, I had been a long-time member of the grief club. Painful memories had ripped opened wounds and now, following the death of my son by his own hand, I am told, "*I can have the gun.*" The gun that he found, the gun that he used to take away his life, could now... be mine. What kind of crazy world were we living in?

I was finally learning that the loss of a child is unlike any other death.

"*... a backpack with Crayolas in it and a 9 millimeter gun with bullets.*"

I took down the information from the police. Then I hung up the phone, sat down... and wailed. Every time I thought that I had found the depths of despair, somehow a deeper layer of pain and misery would reveal itself to me.

Crayons, a gun, and bullets. What a surreal vignette. This was a combination that made no sense to me.

Why do our children pick up, let alone possess guns? Several days after Chris's death, I had asked his friends if they knew he had a gun, and about ten of them said, "Yes." Surprisingly, not one of them thought it was out of the ordinary for another teenager to have a gun, and no one wanted to *snitch* on him either. Ah, yes, the code of the young: *Thou shalt not snitch.* I wondered if any of them had ever wished that they had.

Chris's friends told me that they'd been horsing around and he'd unlatched the passenger-side door of an unlocked parked car to take a couple of CDs... and that's when he found the gun. He'd only had it about three days before he used it. I was surprised as one would never think about a gun being stored in a car in such an upscale community as Scottsdale, AZ.

It's hard to fathom that a prankish teen theft led to pulling a trigger and ending a life. What if? *What if....*

It was a gun that had placed Christopher into the court system at the age of 14. He had been in a car with three other boys. The driver was 18, illegally had a gun in the glove compartment, and was on probation for drug issues. Christopher was the youngest in the car. When they were stopped by a traffic cop who searched the car, Christopher, who had the least to lose, claimed that the gun was his.

He was placed in juvenile detention, where many of his teenage issues caught up with him. He went before a female judge who was very compassionate concerning my trials and attempts as a mother to get Christopher's life turned around. He was having a lot of trouble within the public school system and I was fighting a losing battle to keep his attendance up.

At the time there were many gang members in Arizona and he seemed to be a *"wanna be"* gang member. I explained my dilemma to the judge. So, instead of serving time in the juvenile system she placed him in a residential program for troubled youth for the term of 18 months.

It was there where he not only turned his life around, but where he also matured into an amazing human being. I had been very involved with him in the program and thought that we had walked through fire together and had finally emerged into a life that we would now live happily as family once again.

I believe he should have been followed from that sheltered program by a counselor who would assist him in making his significant life choices as well as a transition program which would have prepared him for the newness of who he was... and to handle the world that he'd left behind. Yet, there never seems to be any money budgeted for such programs.

To offer support during my grieving, my good friend Robert Miley called. A prominent artist living and working in Arizona, he was dedicated to enacting social change, primarily through creativity. We'd worked together for several years, long before Christopher's death, having served on the board of directors of a nonprofit organization that he'd founded, a project he'd designed known as *Release the Fear*. The mission of the project was to counter the effects of violence in our communities by turning fear, anger, and hate into acceptance, hope, and empowerment by bridging varied possibilities through the creative process.

A towering public art sculpture was designed and made from weapons used in violent crimes. Four tons of handguns, machine guns, knives, and more, all confiscated by police, were melted down to build a 24-foot figure with arms outstretched, reaching skyward. Robert wanted to give those touched by violent crime a place to transform their tragedy through art. Though completed in 2005, the sculpture, located in downtown Phoenix, continues to gain national attention as it underscores the highly controversial gun-control debate. City officials, including mayors across the country, have taken notice of the powerful project and its mission.

Robert was saddened that after all the work we had done to seek solutions that would change the world of violence with guns, here we were, dealing with it on my own doorstep. Robert reminded me, "Caara, I know it's painful, but remember this program of *Release the Fear* is about turning pain into possibilities." It was a project of Robert's heart, that of taking art into schools to find ways to release the heartache of children who had lost a loved one by a gun. Many times I would reflect on the crayons in Christopher's backpack. He loved to write and draw.

I asked Robert if he would pick up the gun Christopher used and incorporate it into the statue. He said he would.

I wondered, *Who owned the gun? Why had they left it in their car? Why hadn't they claimed it?*

Six months later I would receive another call from the police department. This time they told me someone had claimed the gun and picked it up. Stunned, I called Robert to see why he had not picked it up. He said softly, "I couldn't, Caara. I care for you too much and feel your pain. So, I asked someone else to retrieve it and they hadn't yet done it."

I've always wondered if anyone had ever thought to tell the gun's owner how it had been used. How would the person feel if he knew that it had been used by a teenage boy to commit suicide? I've always wondered why he took so long to claim it. I wonder about the loose ends within our justice system. In Phoenix, at the time of this writing, you can carry a loaded gun without a permit. It seems evident that new legislation enacted by the state and/or country would help. Shockingly, statistics from the Centers for

Disease Control and Prevention show that each day in America, 14 people under the age of 19 die in gun-related incidents. Yes, <u>each day</u>.

Gun-related deaths for Americans age 14 and under are twelve times that of kids in all other industrialized nations combined. This should be deemed a crisis. Not even after the 1999 Columbine High School massacre or the 2007 Virginia Tech tragedy has any federal law been passed to save children's lives.

It seems not a week goes by that either the television news, or the Internet, cite some horrific, senseless shootings. Don't our kids need to be protected by stricter waiting periods to buy guns, enhanced background checks, and regulations in the secondary market? At one point, I heard that mandatory child safety locks were proposed. Well, my goodness, why not? Proponents to bear arms often argue the 2nd amendment—the right to bear arms, but does that right extend to private citizens or was the law intended to apply to well-regulated militia?

I wonder.

RELEASE THE FEAR
By Robert Miley

A 24' x 8' x 2' statue comprised of a melted
down collected weapons used in violent
crimes. This is the touchstone of grass roots
anti-violence program founded by Arizona
artist Robert J. Miley. Located on Central Ave.
at Roosevelt in downtown Phoenix.

Melted guns from a buyback program similar to the guns in this photo were used by Robert Miley to create the work of art on the previous page, entitled *Release the Fear.*

• Twelve •

Heartbeats In Sync

At times, there was no way for me to describe my feelings of despair. Phone calls came now and then, people stopped by, but I could not engage with any one of them. At one point, my friends would call and I'd just let the phone ring. I didn't answer because I couldn't speak, since no words were there for me to call on. I could only think about Christopher's heart. I wanted to hear it beat.

One moment in time had forever changed my life. Admittedly, the person I knew myself to be had disintegrated. Nothing would ever be the same. Even though I could go back and ask, *why...* a thousand times, I couldn't contemplate any tiny gesture or act that would have changed the course of events that night. But who knows if anything could have made an impact? And none of this searching, wondering, or contemplation would place Christopher back in my arms.

I remember thinking... *I don't know who I am anymore, but I do know I will never be the person I was. The Caara people knew, Christopher's momma, went with him to the grave.*

I could blame, accuse, or point my finger, but the truth of the matter was that Christopher pulled the trigger. And he was gone.

Yet his heart still beats, almost in sync with my own.

My emotions were fierce and erratic. I felt angry with the police for locking me up in the back of the police car on the way to the hospital (what a long, lonely, and frightening ride that had been). I was furious with the owner of the gun, and even upset with Chris's friends for not snitching. I read that anger, following the loss of a loved one, fortifies the bereft to survive, to move forward. Well in that case I'd certainly created a lot of locomotive steam to help me endure. Yet I found myself in an unexpected battle for my own life as the wondering and reliving were creating a situation that was crushing my will to live.

Days passed...
then weeks...
one tough moment at a time.

Honestly, I was just existing... just remaining alive. Replacing the condolence cards came news that caused more pain:

- *An invitation for Christopher to join the marines.*
- *Letters from school.*
- *The ambulance bill.*
- *A hospital bill for $27,000.*
- *A letter from the court citing that Christopher missed his appearance for a traffic ticket.*

• *Thirteen* •
Messages and Reflections

Behind the day-to-day din of my life, as if intuiting a distant, rhythmic, drumming, I heard the ever-present beat of my child's heart. I wrote letters to Brave Heart, telling her how healthy her heart was. I wanted her to know how I had watched to keep his physical body healthy. Introducing him to herbs, healthy eating and exercising.

While I'd still not heard anything from her, I knew that someday I would. I'd sent cards and pictures of both Christopher and our family to help make her aware of her connection to our world.

Creating this montage of my child's life brought back many memories. I often recalled significant events and vivid moments of Christopher's life that kept him alive in my mind and heart. I envisioned his face- heard his laughter- watched him sleeping in my arms. He was such a cute child with very curly hair and grew into a very charming, caring person.

I remembered a day that I looked out my kitchen window and saw him at age three, with his head laying on the handlebars of his tricycle, fast asleep. It was a brand new tricycle that he so loved. Then there was the graduation to a bicycle, when his father and I watched his first try, then his success of riding without training wheels.

For hours I sat in the stands and watched him play little league baseball. How excited he was the first day he got a football uniform in the 7th grade.

His one obsession was shoes. He took such good care of his tennis shoes, carefully cleaning them every night at days end. I was going to miss our love of shopping for those shoes. I would really miss how he would wrap his arm around me as we walked through the shopping center. I would miss the endless nights of doing homework together. Even when I was working out of the country, he would fax me his homework.

Moments of the heart and memory would now be all that I would have from a boy's life. The recording of the words of the heart would now have to whisper to me, "it was a good life." How ironic that he had begun talking and planning about a career in the recording industry. He loved writing rap songs and wanted to have his own recording studio. I wish I could hear, once again, the songs of his life.

• Fourteen •
Words From Beyond

I continued seeking answers that would help tone down my grief. Were there any omens or signs that might have foretold this horrific event? Through the hazy hours of my days, a memory surfaced... I remembered attending a class at Barnes & Noble that had been taught by a friend of mine, Anne Puryear, who wrote a book (entitled *Stephen Lives!*) about her son's death by suicide. It's an inspirational account of the author's 15-year-old son, the message which intends to transform the lives of troubled teens and bring comfort to the families of suicide victims.

She called the class *"1-800 Heaven"* and was teaching us how to do something called "automatic writing," as a way of communicating with those who had "crossed over," and Stephen had communicated with Anne from beyond in this very manner. For this process we were instructed to write our questions with our right hand, while we were taught to write the answers with our left hand. For me, this was a very powerful process.

Anne had worked for 25 years with the Edgar Cayce Foundation in Virginia, and was purported to be a clairvoyant, as well as someone who could read auras. (Cayce was a widely-known psychic with a devoted following, who was reputed to intuit answers to questions about past lives and the future.)

I had heard about Anne's clairvoyant gifts from many friends and even though she wasn't doing aura readings anymore, I had asked Anne to do a reading for Christopher when he was 13, four years prior to his death. During the reading, she saw a red color around him with a hole at his temple. She was puzzled by it and when I brought it up to her after Christopher's death, unfortunately she didn't remember a single thing about the reading.

Yet, I remembered it well. The area where she had seen the hole was the area of his temple where the bullet had entered his skull. Was it a foretelling? It certainly seems to be so.

Beginning with the sacred "visitation" in Christopher's car, on that night of his tragic suicide, and all the way through processing my pain (and ultimately healing my grief), I came to witness and believe that other forces are at play apart from the ones that we see. Behind the visible is a divine play. While to me, life still remains a mystery, I now firmly believe in an otherworldly dimension... and a host of synchronicities among people, places, and things support my theory, discrediting any constructs to the contrary.

Skeptics might claim that I am seeking meaning out of my pain, and I must admit that they'd not be wrong! Indeed, I would much rather find meaning among my life, and the lives of others, rather than see the world as being a realm of random chaos. My experiences after Christopher's death, and the many ways in which the world allowed me to heal, have offered me—and continue to provide— "coincidences" as divine gifts.

The gratitude that I feel for this new "in-sight" is both very deep and profoundly real. I have come to see that revelations do come from pain, and that grace does sweep in enabling clarity. It is the school of hard knocks that no one I know enrolls in willingly. Once in the curriculum, you can't skip any assignments and you must do all of your homework. Furthermore, you must pass all of your tests, and because of that, it isn't easy to graduate! This book is my way of sharing all that I have learned with you... and it is my prayer that it helps you to firmly grab onto hope, as hope is sometimes all that anyone has to hold on to.

I believe that the knowingness that emerges from darkness is the light we all need. As I read the newspaper, search the Internet, or watch TV, there seems to be a constant stream of tragedies, one after the next, each and every day, that simply seem to get worse with the passing of time. There is too much shadow—the light can hardly be seen. My "education" has shown me that within each of us, no matter how veiled by pain or grief, a tiny light is always present just waiting to emerge, enlarge, and emanate. Be especially sure to be around those who are brightly shining their light when yours is dim as it is easy to see bright light and feel the warmth and comfort of the sun in others, so to speak.

Also, trust your intuition when seeking company. Read inspirational stories such as this one or others like it... narratives that celebrate the eclipse of the shadow. People are incredibly resilient. We are made that way. It's in our DNA. Never give up hope. There is always a way.

Other "signs" led my way... in particular, I'm thinking of the eulogy for Christopher. It seems to be a mother's role that since I brought him into the world that I should stand there for him at the end. Even though I stood before an audience of over 300 people, looking back at it now, I really don't know how I did it. I think I was partly on overdrive— adrenaline—and partly numb— the meds! I was surprised that the church was full as there had only been three days to prepare.

For the service I'd created a video of his life and for its background soundtrack, I chose the song, "The Circle of Life," and I saw in the audience so many who had played a part in Christopher's own unique circle of life.

In my numbness, I had not realized that there would be no rush to a service when there is no body to view. I am certain that had I taken more time, and allowed the news of his death to disseminate through the groups of kids that he knew, that there would have been many more in attendance. Yet, I was in awe that so many had chosen to attend. Somehow through the billows of fog, I vaguely remember that Ross spent hours on the phone calling from my phone book.

The services were over and the sisters of the church had prepared food for a dinner. While I wanted to go around to each table to thank all of those who attended, instead I was met by one of Christopher's best friends, Ron. He and his mother were breathless as they were unable to easily find the church and were anxious that they'd missed the service. So, instead of going around to each table, we quickly found a small room so that I could show Ron, who was now crying and quite shaken, the memorial tape. It seems that he'd learned, only moments before, that his friend was dead. His upset was enough that I went to find a psychologist friend, Carl, as Ron was saying that, with Christopher gone, he really didn't want to live.

The suicide of a friend or loved one can often trigger these same kinds of thoughts in those who were close to the victim.

As soon as the tape finished, Ron told his mother that he "needed to go do something." She asked us to wait for them as they would come back, yet it wasn't long before everyone began to leave and the church was soon empty except for Carl, Ross, and me. We lingered a while until we realized they were probably not coming back.

I walked outside the church and glanced up at the sky. Rising out of the blue there was a huge "X" scrawled across the sky. Christopher never left me a note or wrote me a letter without putting "X"s and "O"s on it. I believe that it was his "private" signature message to me on that day, letting me know he was there with me.

Later Ron's mother called to tell me she was sorry they didn't come back. "We were in the park the boys used to hang out in, and when Ron looked up in the sky he saw this giant 'X'," she said.

"He said 'Mom, I'm okay,' and pointing to the 'X' in the sky, he continued by saying, "That's a signal from Christopher!"

For both of us, that "X' was a sign that everything would be okay. But for me, there was still more to come.

When we got home that day I walked to the house through the garage. Christopher's car wasn't home yet as his brother Brian had picked it up from the scene the night of Chris's death and taken it to his house. As I walked into the empty space where his car would have been, there on the cement floor, written in chalk, were the words, "*I love you Mom, X's and O's.*"

Several days before Chris died, Ross had been frustrated because he thought Chris had written some gang writings on the concrete floor. He asked me to ask Chris to erase then, so I said that I would. Yet, when I asked Chris to erase whatever it was that he'd written on the garage floor, he laughed and said, "Mom those aren't gang marks!" He had a very creative way of writing that looked like he'd actually written upside down. In all of the busyness of the past few days, I hadn't looked in the garage until that very moment, having returned from the memorial. There on the floor was another message from Chris... *"I love you Mom, X's and O's."*

Since then, X's have become one of the expressions that I believe are signs that Christopher would whisper to me through the veil.

• *Fifteen* •
Between the Miracles

It had been almost 90 days since Christopher's death and I had finally progressed beyond merely counting the hours and days. Taking life a day at a time, I realized that death had given me a gift as I was learning to "live in the now."

Yet, still grieving, it was often tough just to get dressed each morning, so to make it easier on myself, I wore my large black cotton sweater almost every day. Not only did every part of my body ache, but my skin felt raw as well. The sweater in some small way helped to soothe my body. Maybe someone should invent "healing clothes". They could sew on small tags that warn others that an aching heart *resides within.*

Christopher's Arizona Drivers License. Note the entry for organ donor.

This is my favorite photo of Christopher taken on the Oregon Coast. While I lost many of my photo files, I still have them printed in a book that I made. This photo lacks sharpness due to the source.

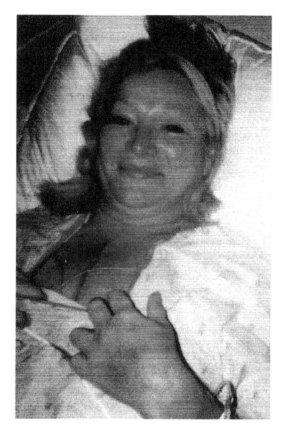

This is a picture of Karen soon after she received Christopher's heart. If you look closely you can see the scar up the center of her chest.

This picture was taken the day that Karen and I first met. Notice the puffiness in her face. This was due to all of the anti rejection medications that she was given to keep her body from rejecting the heart. She now looks much more slender and very beautiful.

Andrea Ward (left), the cranialsacral therapist who worked with Karen (right) and was instrumental in the deeper healing of her heart.

Here I am with Jon Ward, Andrea's husband and a marvelous benefactor who provided the way for Andrea, Karen, and I to go to Florida for our work with Dr. Upledger.

Brian Dean Holliday

My son and older brother of Christopher. Until I began writing this book I didn't realize how inter-twined their lives had been and would become even more so through this journey of the heart.

Christopher outside the Mormon Temple in Mesa, AZ
in December of 1994. Notice his pose of giving.

Karen on her trip to Canada which caused her to miss
her first transplant. Notice how happy she is in her
pose of receiving, in spite of missing her first
opportunity at receiving a new heart.

Karen and "Mr. Bill," on their wedding day in Prescott, AZ.

• Sixteen •
God's Wise Masters of Life

I sought every way that I knew to feel connected to my lost son. Studies show that those who lose a loved one want ways to continue to feel a true bond with the deceased. In April, almost three months after Christopher's death, I finally touched Christopher's ashes, sticking my hand into the urn as if it contained rich soil. I wailed as I felt the tiny fragments of his bones. Then I touched my lips with the smooth ash and remembered the oneness of our spirits.

I sought distraction, as well. One of the best things that had happened during those first few months was that I'd acquired a computer, and it would become my best friend. Not only was the computer a great resource, but it also brought me much comfort. In an effort to drown out the ticking of the clock, and fill the agonizing silence, I wrote every day and as I did, I found my writing to be healing. In the midst of my writing I continued to often think about the

49-year-old woman who had received Christopher's heart and yearned for the day that I would meet her. Once again hugging the heart that I had birthed was a vision that I daily held.

In June, seven months after Christopher's passing, we gave up our house and took a trip, first to California, and then Oregon, before relocating to Denver. We'd been thinking of moving and now it seemed that a new set of surroundings might serve as a strong component to aid in alleviating my pain, and Denver also offered the promise of a business opportunity. I was eager to return to my roots and the environs of Christopher's birth.

Over the next several weeks we packed and prepared to leave, while again, I sorted through Christopher's clothes and belongings. I had called my friend Carl, whom Christopher had loved, and asked him if he would keep Christopher's ashes for a while. He said that he would. The rest of his things I put safely in storage, along with other odds and ends, before leaving for a month to San Diego. Ross put Christopher's urn in a beautiful Easter basket and placed it on the front seat of the car, secured by the seatbelt.

Again, we followed that familiar road that we'd travelled so many times together as we went to visit Christopher in the residential facility, where he'd lived for 18 months. Carl's house was on the way. It was just months before that that Christopher and I had gone together to Carl's house. How poignant—seeing these two journeys side-by-side...how different this ride.

Even though Christopher's physical body had been reduced to ashes, here I was, returning it to the care of someone who'd been with him in human form for nearly every day over eighteen months. Carl, a psychologist who'd become a lifetime friend, had turned Christopher's life around. For eight hours, often in silence and in prayer, he sat with me at the hospital bedside... anticipating these unimaginable words, "*He is now brain dead.*"

I don't think there can be a more intimate, unspoken experience as friends than to have shared a moment such as this. I would now entrust Carl with all that was left of the boy we'd both loved, with what had become sacred ashes. In my mind, this still seemed to be so surreal.

The Red Rocks Chapel in Sedona, Arizona where there are memorials to both of my sons.

· *Seventeen* ·

Bridged

We spent a month overlooking the ocean in the lovely San Diego home of a dear friend. Lingering at the shore as I watched the waves roll in enabled me to see and feel how much bigger the world is than me. I felt humbled as I witnessed signs of birth, death, and rebirth all around... whether rotted trees that decomposed to enhance soil for new growth, or various abandoned shells where life had once taken root and grown. The apparent cycles infused me with the knowledge that life is an exquisite circle—a path taken by all throughout the whole of history.

We can only walk the long road doing the best we can with whatever we encounter. This epiphany gave me courage and strength to endure, as well as release judgment for all. Attuned with the natural world, I could feel that love reigned. The tranquility of the ocean and the vast beach quieted my racing thoughts, allowing me to see that love—the heart—was the beat beneath everything.

My friend seemed to know that this vacation would give us the rest and shift of perspective that we needed before embarking on the next leg of our journey as well as in heading to our final destination... Denver, Colorado where I'd be working with another friend of mine. At one time I had actually been the recruiter for the company he worked for, and then he had managed a company of mine for two years in Vancouver B.C. From there, I'd negotiated him getting his own location in Denver, and now my friend wanted to return the favor by offering me the opportunity to work for a while in the field I knew so well... the field of inventions, or the field of new possibilities and beginnings.

He too, felt that a change of location would help me handle my grief. I was soon to learn that most others felt that just getting busy would ease the pain. What no one seemed to understand was that Post Traumatic Stress had now become my constant companion. While at times it spoke quietly, there were times when it roared loudly. Even though I knew this companion sat in my brokenness, I didn't yet know its name.

My life partner Ross and his eight year old daughter, Avalon, set out for Denver from San Diego, while I headed north to take my granddaughter, Kimberly, back to Seattle and to her father... my second born son Brian. She'd spent the summer with us and now it was time for her to return home to family, school, and her own life. Our journey north would take us through the parts of Oregon that I grew up in, the land of the Myrtle tree.

It was in the small village with the name "Bridge," the town where I grew up, that I received the gift I had been waiting for. I was staying there for a few days with my cousin. Out of hopefulness, I'd kept my phone connected to a voicemail service while I was on the road. I really didn't know if or when I'd get the call, but I wanted to be prepared in the event that I did. Finally the veil of life between the physical and the spiritual was bridged by a melodic voice that said, "This is Karen. I received Christopher's heart. Please call me".

I was breathless. Listening to the voice mail over and over again, I finally knelt and cried... and gave thanks. Christopher's heart had finally found me.

I was so overwhelmed with emotion that I wasn't able to call her back immediately. I first needed to integrate the knowing that, somewhere in time, Christopher had reached out to me, and found me in the mountains of Oregon... where I'd been a little girl and where I had grown up. He'd found me alright, here at the heart of my childhood memories; in the land that bore my first footprints, and the land that smelled of the fragrant flowers of the Myrtle tree.

Karen and I, both having endured long and painful journeys over the bridge, would now meet in the middle. We would have so much to share. The bond between a mother and her child, maybe life's strongest connection, was bridged once again.

I knew how much Ross was struggling with Christopher's death in his own way. Most know that the loss of a child, particularly by suicide, brings stress like no other and is one of those "top-of-the-list" stressors.

Statistics document that most couples don't survive it. Like many women, I was attuned to my partner's feelings... to his struggles. I had a deep-rooted suspicion that wouldn't cease; a continual pulling on my sleeve that told me Ross was leaving me, and that this was the beginning of the end.

It had been almost six months since Christopher had taken his life. I wondered if Ross wanted out but felt this was an acceptable time to leave? Yet with six months having passed this also meant that Brave Heart might be nearing the receipt of permission to connect with me. There is no way to prove that I intuited that her contacting me was fast approaching. I understand that it's a stretch to say that I heard the heart.

But, well, there it is, I said it.

Eighteen

The Call and Meeting
of the Hearts

Before I could honor this momentous occasion and return the call to Karen I wanted to ground myself in the earthy forest of Oregon. I felt that "heaven had called" and that the spirit of Christopher had whispered to me from beyond. It was to be one of many more signposts on this journey that evidenced how thin this veil is between physical and spirit.

My heart was feeling the anticipation of a new birth, "a rebirth." Suddenly, I had the memory of the moment he was born, remembering how fast the pain had left after his birth. While I was exhausted from the birth of grief, I now anticipated the joy of this sudden reconnection, and the anticipation of a new journey with the heart I had birthed in a boy.

With my granddaughter Kimberly now in Seattle, I headed over the mountains to Denver in Christopher's little white Geo Tracker. I loved his little car and would forever hold the knowledge that we took our last ride to his place of departing in this car. As I drove up and over a mountain that night into a small town in Wyoming called Casper, the brightness of the full moon cast a magical light over the darkness of the night. I felt the presence of angels by my side and felt as though they'd brought the stars within my reach.

A golden glow emanated from windows within the sweet houses that lined the blocks of this small town. I recall seeing a front porch strung with the muted tones of paper lanterns reminding me that even the thinnest veil can diminish one's light. The radio whispered love songs. I turned up the volume and sang the phrases I heard to my son as I imagined Chris singing along. We often sang together on long rides. I missed him so much.

Chris loved song lyrics and was intrigued by unusual names and their symbolism. Interestingly, my Christopher had chosen to rename himself *Casper* in the year before he died. We had even changed his name on his school records. Now I wondered, was this yet another omen, that on some level he knew he would eventually only be with me in spirit? He had died under the full of the moon, and so it was on this night that I looked at the full moon as the symbol of a new beginning.

It was in this town of Casper, Wyoming where I decided to return the call to the heart that had reached out to me.

Checking into a small motel, I knelt and prayed before picking up the phone. Her voice resonated in my heart. I remembered the first ultrasound during my pregnancy with Christopher, when I heard the beat of this heart that had now taken on a new and wondrous mission.

Over the next three months, Karen and I shared many conversations. We marveled at how we were both looking and waiting for one another. We'd exchanged information about our lives. While she was adjusting to her new heart, and her new life, I was living with a broken heart. How I'd wished that I, too, could have had a transplant.

We'd spoken many times, and now Karen and I were finally ready to meet one another, finally choosing Thanksgiving Day to mark the occasion. Like many, I've always associated the holiday with joy and union. Of course, it is a day to remind us to count our blessings—especially while grieving—and be "at one" with those celebrating. It seemed the perfect day to greet the heart. Yet, my emotions were all jumbled: excitement, sadness, gratitude, even fear. Having a dream come true is sometimes a lot to handle!

I would fly from Colorado to meet her in Phoenix, Arizona. My dear friend, Donna, would pick me up at the airport, as I was too nervous to rent a car or to drive to Karen's house. I envisioned a neutral place for this meeting of the "heart".

Somehow, nine months had now passed since Christopher's passing. It wasn't lost on me that this was also the time that it takes to carry and give birth to a child. Surviving the death of a loved one is not unlike the labor of birth, except in place of the delivery, there's just a softening of the pain. Even though the transplant agency had suggested we give it a year before contacting one another, they felt that we were ready since we were both making such an effort. I felt gratitude that we were given this grace.

During this time, as I had suspected, my relationship with Ross was coming to an end. Sadly, our days had been numbered by the attempt to survive this tragedy. Not only was I no longer the woman he'd known, nothing would ever be the same.

The family fight that fateful night that sent Christopher and me out of the house was typical of many teenage fights. It was one of those fights where voices are raised and things are spoken in haste.

In my heart, I didn't blame Ross, although I know my actions often said things differently. I felt compassion for him. It's been said that 80-percent of marriages end in divorce within one year of the death of a child. Christopher was not his child, and I was not his wife, although we had lived together four years as husband and wife, yet in that capacity he'd been very good to Christopher. It's not easy to take on a new relationship with a 13-year-old boy who's going through puberty.

One time when Christopher was angry with Ross, I asked him what was wrong. Christopher replied, "Mom, I wouldn't like any man you were with." The boy always wants to be the man of the house.

Nineteen

Heart to Heart

I was arriving to this momentous meeting with both a heavy and excited heart. In our conversations, Karen had told me many times that she no longer looked like she had before receiving the heart. She was no longer a size six, having gained 100 pounds from the steroid medication, Prednisone, which she had to take, as well as a lack of exercise for fear of over-exerting her new heart.

We had decided to meet at my friend's house and as I opened the door to greet Karen, my body was shaking. The first thing I noticed were her vivid, sky blue eyes. My mind immediately retraced a moment in Christopher's childhood, when he'd brought home a piece of artwork that he'd made in school, something he wanted me to have. He had created a beautiful cardboard mask that he'd painted with sky blue eyes encircled by brown.

I asked my brown-eyed Christopher, "Why did you make brown eyes with a blue center?"

He smiled and said, "I don't know, just felt like it."

And now, here I was, welcoming his heart in a new form, with sky blue eyes.

For a brief moment I felt the earth stand still.

Karen and I sat and talked for hours. In my overwhelmed state of mind, I could tell that she knew I had a grieving heart. She had one child, a 14-year-old boy named Justin. She told me that her motivation to live was her desire to see her son graduate from high school—that she knew he wouldn't make it without her. Her life as a single mother had been difficult and Justin was very dependent upon her.

I only heard bits and pieces of the stories she was telling me, as somewhere in the greater universe, angels were holding me. We decided that the next day I would meet the rest of the family, her fiancé and only son.

On this night, I would cocoon in bed with the knowing that in the greater scheme of life, something good had happened in the midst of a great tragedy. I was to remember that the Bible says there are many things in this lifetime that we would not have the answer to, and this was certainly one of them. And it also says, for every time there is a season... this was the season of the heart.

Later my friend, Donna, told me that she felt as though she was "witnessing something magical." She knew the suffering of my heart, but on a deeper level we both believed that Christopher and I had chosen... somewhere in time... to give a gift. It was called: *the gift of life.*

I'd met Karen during Thanksgiving season, and it eased my pain to realize that I was sitting with Christopher's heart on that first Thanksgiving without him. I was so thankful that someone had breathed life into his heart. It was so comforting to know that his heart was still upon planet earth, and even more comforting that it had been a gift.

• Twenty •

Come Home

Soon it was Christmas—the first Christmas after Christopher's leaving and my mind drifted back to the previous year. While Christopher had spent his last Christmas in Seattle with his father, he hadn't wanted to be there, as he'd wanted to be with his girlfriend Jessica; the girl who had won his heart at the age of 13.

For what seemed to them to be an eternity, they had been apart because she had been sent by her family to a military school in New Mexico, while Christopher had spent 18 months in a residential rehab program for teens. They'd only recently been in the same city and in his heart he was afraid he was going to lose her again, as there was a young man who was now in college coming to visit her in Arizona over the Christmas season. She and this boy had both known one another in military school.

Ross and I were going to Denver to be with his family and Christopher hadn't seen his father in a long time. So the decision was made that Christopher would go to Seattle. Christopher called me every day in Denver, begging me to fly him from Seattle back to Arizona. I finally sent him home one day early. The heart of a seventeen-year-old young man is very fragile in the department called "love". Was this a piece of the puzzle that brought about the rash decision that he'd made?

So this year, while Ross went to Kansas to be with his family, I chose to spend Christmas in Seattle. I hadn't wanted to go with Ross, as after Christopher had died, I had a challenging time with his family. It felt as though they just expected me to get over my grief and move on. So I chose not to celebrate with them. In doing so, somehow I knew that I was sending Ross off, never to return.

My intuition turned out to be right. Ross must have told his family that our relationship had come to an end. His sister-in-law fixed him up with a blind date and he fell in love.

He'd found a younger woman, a woman without children, and even more poignant... one without grief.

It seems that loss is never well-timed. I've often wondered how Ross could've left me on my first Christmas without my son. January 5th would be the first anniversary of Christopher's passing. He later reminded me that I had been leaving on the night Christopher died. And actually I was.

On that very day I had rented an apartment for Christopher and me to move into. Ross was right... I had been the first one to leave. However, after we'd moved to Denver, I sought counseling to find tools to keep our relationship together. I had lost Christopher and I didn't want to lose Avalon, too, especially as I had been with her for five years.

Since we were already on shaky ground, it was probably just a matter of time before my relationship with Ross would eventually have crumbled, regardless of the effort either one of us put forth. I couldn't blame him for his concern for his daughter Avalon being around my grief, nor could I truly blame his family for supporting his desire to leave.

Couples often encounter a number of saboteurs while dealing with grief. Often times a lack of communication drives a wedge between them, especially if they are polarized in their feelings. Differences in the ways each partner grieves can create stress, and in many cases, blame and guilt also play a part. If a couple had problems before a child's death, as was our case, those problems can become even more difficult to deal with in the aftermath.

After Christmas, I faced the New Year alone. I became so despondent that I actually thought of committing suicide myself. I was still so raw. I have since read studies that show more than 33,000 people take their own lives each year, and in doing so, leave behind survivors who struggle to make sense of a senseless death. Just as depression is often the underlying cause of suicide, especially the suicide of a child, depression can take hold. In fact, survivors themselves are at risk of suicide ideation. If you're a survivor of suicide, or the death of a child, and you find yourself feeling this way, please contact the Suicide Hotline in your area. I've provided you with this number at the back of this book.

Despite my best efforts I was soon to "lose" another child, Ross's daughter, Avalon, who was now nine-years-old. While grieving the loss of Christopher I'd drawn even closer to her. She too, would lose me, her second mother. As I packed my clothes I told her that I would be back, as I truly wanted to believe that Ross had only needed a break.

As I gathered my things, I sat on the floor crying. The phone rang, it was Karen... it was Christopher's heart, asking me, what's wrong? I told her Ross had wanted me to leave. She asked, "Where are you going?"

I responded, "I don't know."

There was a silence and then she said softly, "Come home Caara, come home."

So I did.

This is me with Christopher in 1996. All dressed up
with somewhere to go.

• Twenty One •
Heart and Spirit

It was the middle of a bitter cold winter when I got into Christopher's little Geo Tracker to begin the drive back to Arizona. I'd written down the directions, as I wasn't familiar with the area in which Karen lived.

Getting off the freeway, I stopped at the first traffic light where something felt very familiar. I suddenly realized that I was right at the corner where Christopher had shot himself. I was at 19th Avenue and Bell Road, near the parking lot of the Big Five Sporting Goods store.

My heart leaped. *Big Five...* As had happened on other occasions, a memory began to take form when I saw the number, *"five."* I remembered that as a little boy of four, Christopher would give everyone "a high five," something that his brother, Brian, had taught him to do. Instead of being sad in that moment, I was comforted, feeling that this was another sign from Christopher, telling me that life would be okay... a "high five from heaven."

Karen had unknowingly moved only a few blocks from where Christopher had shot himself. We had all lived in Scottsdale when he died--so close, without knowing the whereabouts of one another. Karen had loved tacos and had often eaten at the same restaurant Christopher and I used to go to. It was remarkable to think that at some point we could have all been in the same restaurant eating at the same time. We would later find out that there was more truth to this than either of us realized.

Christopher's little Geo Tracker was not the vehicle he would have chosen, but it was economical and sporty looking. I pulled into the driveway of Karen's house and there sat another Geo Tracker. It was the same exact style in red - another synchronistic happening. We both smiled and named Christopher's car, *Spirit...* and hers (being red), we named *Heart.*

I had arrived at Karen's front door, raw in form beyond words. Not only was my son gone, but now my relationships with Ross and Avalon were absent from my life; another immeasurable loss. What was truly keeping me alive at this point in time was the desire to nurture the heart.

It was not an easy entry as Karen, too, was going through

her own loss. She was grieving the loss of her own heart, one that had served her for 49 years.

Here we were, two women, grieving yet grateful. I walked into Karen's life as if I had always been there and we both began a new journey; the journey of the heart. And now that heart had called out... "*Come home.*" As far as my research has taken me, I have yet to discover another similar co-habitation: The heart donor's mother and the heart's recipient. It would reveal itself as a unique, kind, and giving relationship. Karen and I helped each other heal, as we continue to do so 17 years later. As close as any sisters could be, we coined ourselves a sisterhood, and while we no longer live under the same roof, we are still family through and through.

So many emotions required careful processing. Grief certainly took center stage. Karen grieved her lost "self"— the healthy woman before all the heart problems she endured and the arduous road to recovery. Of course, I grieved my son. Yet, in gifting his organs, I received a gift. Chris did not vanish completely as his heart—and other organs—still live helping others. It felt that Karen, Justin, and I humbly bowed in reverence to the mystery of life— the exquisite human body and its organs, the wondrous ability of the heart to sustain life. Who could not behold the miracle before us? The advances of science—of trailblazing physicians and scientists—had enabled life where tragedy had struck. This was as close to magic as anyone can get.

Both Karen and I were dedicated to emerging into healthy lives, coming together under the most unusual set of circumstances with a common goal--to continue life with faith in love. This was our bond. In doing so, we helped ourselves, one another, and likely the most fulfilling of all, we also helped her son, Justin live a happy and healthy life.

This is Spirit, originally Christopher's little Geo Tracker, but it was also my home for a while as I struggled with the pain of my loss.

• *Twenty Two* •
The Awakening of the Heart

During one of our conversations, Karen was describing what it had been like as she was prepared to receive, and went through, her heart transplant, relating to me that she remembered awakening during surgery. In recent years we've learned that this is not so unusual and is known as a "translucent moment" during an operation. Many surgical patients hear and remember the conversations of their medical teams and Karen had heard her surgeon ask for a trash bag for her heart, or a body parts bag, to use their own "sterile" terminology.

As a result of studies that have been conducted, specifically with heart transplantation, it's been learned that many patients have heard these conversations. For this very reason, some doctors have a nurse who actually sits throughout the procedure and begins an odyssey, talking to the transplant recipient throughout their entire surgery. She will say something like,

"Now they're opening your chest... and they're going to take your heart out"... lovingly guiding the patient through the experience of giving up a heart that had served them for years. If you'd like to read more about this, there's a beautiful story in the book *Heart Codes*, by Paul Pearsall, Ph.D. Among the many things he writes about in this book, the author relates the need to be sensitive to the transplanted heart when it's being taken.

How I wish such a kind soul had been sitting with Karen. As she recounted this experience, she said sadly, "I wanted to bury my heart. It had served me for 49 years." After I heard Karen's story, I wondered if anyone on her medical team had ever thought about the body part that they were throwing away. My curiosity now deepened and wondered, *"what of the heart?"* What of the new heart being transplanted into a new body? What happens to it? Is there any element of recall? I had so many questions about cellular memory and the tearing away of a part of the body.

Together, Karen and I grieved her heart, and my son, each of us reacting very differently to our losses. While she was deeply depressed, often choosing to sit in the dark, I felt highly charged. In hindsight, I'm sure that at the time I was experiencing PTSD (post traumatic stress disorder) and all of its typical symptoms.

It's not unusual for people who've sustained the loss of a child to suffer from PTSD, an emotional illness that has been formally classified as an anxiety disorder. It often develops as a result of a terribly frightening, life-threatening, or otherwise deeply emotional experience. Recognized as a formal diagnosis in 1980, you've probably heard or read about war veterans who suffer from PTSD, as well as victims of abuse or accident. Those who suffer are highly sensitive to normal life experiences, with a state of hyper-arousal being common.

Regardless of our challenging symptoms, Karen and I often met in the middle, both willing to explore the unknown as we offered each other emotional support.

Karen's son Justin and I became immediate friends. I would become his sounding board for life while he would become a new reason for me to live, as he and I began to build a world of dreams together. To this day he still has the very first treasure board I taught him to make. Being only three years younger than Christopher when we met, he allowed me to express the motherly feelings that I'd lost when my own son died.

While still in Denver, after connecting with Karen, I had called upon my friend and healer Andrea Ward. She's a therapist and a faculty member of a prominent school of alternative medicine and healing, Rain Star University, located in Scottsdale. As a university, they not only offer education programs, but therapeutic services as well, including craniosacral therapy, massage therapy, and acupuncture. With my call, I arranged for Andrea to begin working with Karen, as she had assisted my own healing process with great compassion and skill.

Specializing in an increasingly popular healing modality known as craniosacral therapy, Andrea employed this technique with Karen to assist her in regaining her health and relieving her depression. Karen told Andrea that her body had felt odd since the surgery, as if she was a rag doll, unable to own and control her own body. It was the only way she could describe her feeling of disintegration after the surgery. Atop a massage table, the patient fully clothed, a craniosacral therapist applies a light, therapeutic touch to the head, face, and spine, and this bodywork is said to regulate the flow of cerebrospinal fluid. I recall seeing a shift in Karen into health and happiness. Karen integrated that session over several months and often spoke of its power to help her heal.

In a later session, to resolve the sadness she felt about the removal of her heart before the transplantation, she visualized her heart being buried with honor and dignity. She thanked her heart; she really acknowledged it. She forgave the doctors who said that it had no value for scientific study. Then she felt a release and shift. She said instead of feeling dead inside and having a hole in her chest, that she experienced aliveness, now finally welcoming the new heart beating inside her as part of her own body.

Before Christopher's death, I'd been in a network marketing business (within the health/wellness field), and knew many distributors who were in the healing business and embraced natural medicine. Andrea and I knew many healing hands who were willing and skilled to apply therapeutic touch to Karen and her new heart. In addition to Andrea's craniosacral therapy, Karen was also lovingly treated with reiki, massage, reflexology, acupuncture, sacred oils, and many more alternative healing modalities. So very many were willing to work on her, and she was open to having them do so. One intention of this was to reduce her many medications, as many as 50 pills a day. Happily, these efforts were a success.

She was prescribed immunosuppressant drugs to "suppress" her immune system, so that her body would not reject the new heart. Organ rejection is the body's natural defense to transplantation... it is nature's way. The body is on the prowl for anything foreign to the system, such as germs. The body's attempt to reject the organ is a sort of misguided attack to keep the body safe from invasion and harm. It's tricky because while the drugs lower defenses so that the heart will be "accepted," the medicine's effect leaves the patient more vulnerable to infection.

However Karen was open and willing to walk through the fire, to receive any kind of treatment, many of which were actually building her immune system. I believe that her willingness to risk is why she has outlived the projected life span of a heart transplant recipient by twice the number of years, while also being able to cut her medication intake for several years. She truly developed the desire to explore many ways to harmonize her body, mind, and spirit.

It was wonderful to see Karen come out of her depression and display her strength. It didn't take long to discover that she was a warrior. It's traumatic, both emotionally and physically, to receive a new heart. I admire anyone who endures a major organ transplant. Nothing in her life was the same. She'd gone from a size 6 to a size 24. The drugs had made her beautiful slim face swell to such a size, that except for her vivid blue eyes, she looked little if anything like her former self. Yet, as she healed, her beauty and strength began to shine once again.

She was intolerant of the weight gain and longed to be her slender self once again. The prednisone gave her facial hair and masculine traits. She tried hard not to be vain about this, and we often laughed about it a lot. Soon, we were walking together and she learned even more from the healers who served her. She was thirsty for knowledge and began spending hours on the computer, either seeking the resources to accelerate her body's natural ability to heal, or fulfilling her curiosity and joy, even lust, for learning.

As Karen began to explore life with her new heart, she put her newfound energy and long standing creativity into creating websites, even creating a beautiful memorial to Christopher. Long before there any programs that taught people how to make websites, with her incredible talent and intellect, she taught herself how to do this. We marveled at her creations. As she found the pictures and the songs that expressed her "heart," these creations of hers would soothe my own aching heart as well.

Karen had wanted to live to make sure that Justin made it through high school, and he knew the importance of this to her. He worked hard to maintain good grades. Justin never doubted that he would continue on to college. His strength of spirit and commitment not only saw him through high school, he also graduated Summa Cum Laude from Arizona State University.

One day, Karen needed to have a MRI of her heart, so I offered to drive her to the appointment. It was an oppressively hot Arizona summer day... at least 110 degrees outside... and now at her heaviest weight, she was also in a wheelchair. I went to pull her chair out the door, but dropped her and was unable to pick her up. Feeling helpless myself, I could also feel her own humiliation and fragility in knowing that she was too heavy for me to lift. I was in a panic. Afraid to leave her in the heat, even for a minute to go call for help, I couldn't think of anything to do. My body was in Red Alert and my entire system began racing. Soon the neighbor next door pulled into his drive way and I yelled for him to come over. Being stronger than me, he picked Karen up and helped her into the car.

Karen has a wonderful ability to see the humor in almost anything. Out of relief, we laughed all the way to the doctor's office. As she was called into the MRI room, the nurse asked if I was a relative. I said, "Sort of. I birthed the heart you're going to take a picture of."

Her eyes filled with tears, and she asked, "Do you want to see the heart?"

I was overjoyed as the technician allowed me to look into the heart that I'd birthed. Memories surfaced. I recalled when I was pregnant with Christopher, and for the first time heard the beat of his heart as I saw it on the ultrasound screen.

The nurse too, was moved by such an event unfolding in front of her. How often would a nurse meet both the donor mom and the recipient of a heart transplant? I felt the heavens move and I knew again, an angel unaware had served me. As we left, the nurse gave me a copy of the picture of Christopher's heart, and now I had a picture of "life."

Karen and I went to have lunch and we both felt spirit move. How blessed we were in the midst of every day happenings to know that that we were living something very different than most would ever experience. She made a vow that day... to lose weight and celebrate being alive.

Twenty Three

Moving On

I stayed with Karen for nine months, again the time for a child's gestation and birth. There were times when we didn't know if the heart was hers, Christopher's, mine, or ours. Although on occasion it was a challenge for us to be together, the grace in all of it was that we never gave up our new sisterhood, our new friendship... this unknown parallel of universes that we seemed to be traveling within.

While I'd hoped that I'd be going back to Denver, I soon came to the realization that it was not going to be. Thankfully, Ross had allowed Avalon to come out during the summer to visit Karen and me, and Avalon's real mother, Brenda.

When Ross and I became a couple, I was the one who was responsible for bringing Brenda back into Avalon's life, in spite of her continued struggle with addiction. As a meth addict, she continued using even though I had helped to orchestrate her intervention. I knew how much she desired to be a mother to Avalon, but the call of the drug overrode that desire. Now in my own brokenness, It seemed Brenda was now one of the few people who could match the raw energy of my body, so she, in her own dysfunction, helped me to survive. We both suffered the loss of Ross and Avalon in our own ways.

The loss of Avalon after her divorce from Ross had only added to Brenda's struggle with addictions. I was aware of her struggle and had made a pact with her that she could help with Avalon anytime she wanted, as long as she was honest with me, and she was. Later I would apologize to her for helping Ross financially through his divorce as I had paid for his court costs to get sole legal custody of Avalon when she was four. Avalon loved me even more now because I loved her mom, yet she was unaware that soon enough she would lose us both.

When I apologized to Brenda for the part that I'd played in Ross divorcing her, she said, "If God had told me to pick out a new mother for Avalon, I would've picked you." That meant so much to me. Sadly, we now shared broken hearts over the loss of our children.

Nine months after Christopher died, Brenda gave birth to a baby boy. Soon after, she called to ask me if she could name him Christopher. I said, "yes".

Tragically, Brenda died from her addictions and grief at the age of 44. I often prayed for her to be able to reach a place where she could finally begin helping herself, but unfortunately she was unable to do so. She was a beautiful woman and had a zest for life. Her inability to fight the addiction did not take away who she was. It just showed another unfortunate fatality and lifetime heart ache for Avalon to know how powerful and debilitating drugs are.

When I placed Avalon back on the plane to go home to Ross, I knew I wouldn't see her again for a long time. My soul was torn and the depth of my despair grew deeper. I knew it was time for me to leave Karen's house. I truly lived in a dual world of reality and a surreal dreamscape.

In the months of living with Karen, I had given away all my furniture, books, and things that no longer mattered to me. It was all just stuff. I couldn't find the strength to sell it in garage sales, so I called several friends to come and take my things away.

When I finally moved out of Karen's house, no one knew that I really didn't have any place to go. My body was still on super-charge. I had not had any counseling for all of my losses. The post-traumatic stress that I'd suffered after Christopher's death was once more triggered by my recent loss of Ross and Avalon. In hindsight, I can now see that I was barely functioning.

I would spend several weeks living in that little Geo Tracker, "Spirit". I stayed at truck stops where I could shower and somehow felt safe, tucked back against a huge truck whose engine roared... a soothing sound to my companion of PTSD.

I had let go of all my belongings except for my clothing. Christopher's father, Richard had given me a Shell credit card, which I used to buy gas, water, and food. The Geo Tracker was the last thing I had that was Christopher's and it served me well. During this time I seemed to fool everyone, somehow leading them to believe that I was living a normal life.

Eventually with the help of a friend, I managed to live in a small studio apartment. I had gone from earning six figures a year in network marketing to an income of zero, and had now entered a dangerous time in my life, one of living with PTSD. I "handled" it on my own, without therapy, and slowly it became much less my friend and a lot more my enemy. Money would appear from friends, as well as strangers, and help me through those dire times. So many in my life during that time were angels unaware.

While I'd let go of nearly all my material things, I was still unable to let go of my grief and PTSD. I couldn't find the driving successful businesswoman I'd once been. Yet, intuitively, I knew that I had to battle the downward spiral that was happening in my life.

And then it happened...in a single, fleeting moment the one thing that I had of Christopher's was taken from me. I pulled out in front of a Lincoln Town Car that broadsided me, totaling the Tracker. Since this happened near a fire near a fire station, an ambulance arrived almost imme-diately. Even thought I'd been "t-boned," or hit on the side of my door, no matter how bruised I felt, I was not going to leave the car. How could this happen? I wanted to drive that little car until its wheels fell off. In deep grief I cried for three days, not letting the insurance company haul off the car until I could finally allow myself to let it go.

An unaware angel friend gave me a bicycle, so for the rest of the summer I rode the bicycle everywhere; the energy spent riding that bike may have been what kept me alive. Then I met a man who gave me a computer and told me to write my story. Using the skills that I'd learned from Karen, I built a website about grief. Now I was the one staying up all night, wrestling with the demon known as PTSD.

In the aftermath of this experience I gained an incredible amount of sympathy for returning vets, especially those who return from battle zones. Even today, with all the knowledge and support that they have, they too, wrestle with the unknown as they try to handle it themselves... not sharing with anyone any information about this thing that comes and goes.

While I had once battled for the heart, I was now battling for my life. I had received a response on my grief website from a father who had lost his daughter and seemed to understand what was happening to me... and he wanted to help. He told me that he was an artist with a lovely place in Hawaii with an extra room, and invited me to come stay with him for a while. I accepted.

I'd received a check from the insurance company... a pittance for Christopher's Tracker that had been totaled... but it gave me enough to buy the ticket. Yet, first I wanted to attend the wedding of my dear friend, Andrea.

• *Twenty Four* •

Leaving

It was a beautiful summer day in Sedona, Arizona, when Karen and I attended Andrea's wedding, which just happened to include a fire walk and an open house party at the newlyweds' home. Karen and I so admired Andrea and were now eager to partake in her celebration. There we were, all together in the magical setting of the red rocks of Sedona.

The fire walk took place the night before the wedding. In preparation, each one who chooses to walk must first take time to become clear and centered, entering a state in which there is no fear, and therefore, no injury. It was an incredibly sacred experience in time to watch Karen walk across the hot coals. My own heart swelled as I shared in the joy of a warrior woman who had made the choice to defy all odds, for in reality she had already walked the fire of life.

I felt the heavens open and I knew that this would be a new beginning for her, marking a new level of confidence. She most certainly was a warrior and a survivor. However, at this time the same would not be for me, for on this night I could not find that safe place of "knowing" that I could walk without being burned. While I had participated in a fire walk several months prior, this time my life was too fragile, my body too weary, and somehow the voice of fear kept me from walking.

The next day was to be Andrea's open house, yet I was not attending. It was the time to tell my two friends that I was leaving, going to another magical location... a place known as Hawaii.

Anyone would have guessed that deep down, I was really looking for a way to give my life meaning. Having been a child bride, and birthing my first four children so young, Christopher, as my late-in-life child, presented a different kind of parental opportunity for me. I was, admittedly, more present with him as a parent, as I was more grown up myself. Mother-son relationships morph and while we had challenges in his teenage years, we were also close. We were friends and I missed his company, as well as the role that he gave me, that of Mother.

As I spoke, and continued to speak with women who transition from their primary role as a mother into a bigger role within the broader world, I see how challenging it is for someone to reinvent their identity within society and within their own home. By nature, I am a giver, which seems to be the role of most women I know. We like to nurture... to see things grow. Even though men enjoy nurturing, too, throughout history, this has been the predominant role of women. It feels okay to say that nurturing runs through our veins. Karen, Andrea, and I each facilitated growth within one another. Yet I now sought other ways in which to blossom and facilitate my own much-needed growth.

While it was foolish to go to a strange place and stay with a stranger, I had no fear and may have even been somewhat eager to explore danger. Once again, I gave away all of my belongings, leaving only with a suitcase and my computer.

Hawaii was beautiful, the aromas exotic, my host friendly, the ocean welcoming... but it wasn't long before things changed and suddenly I was experiencing full-fledged PTSD... I was in the battlefield and my life was being threatened. Every molecule in me felt the fear of the fire walk and I knew that I must escape this life threatening arrangement.

In a chain of events, I awakened in a shelter for women on the inner island of Oahu, being the only haole' in a home of about twenty Hawaiian women. Daily, women came and went; I was in an unknown world unlike any I had ever been in before or since. The staff loved me, cared for me, sang songs of love to me. No one asked me questions. The director of the program said to me, "I knew you were different when you showed up."

She was the first to recognize that PTSD was a problem for me. Luckily for me, the Veteran's hospital on the island had opened up their testing program for non-military personnel to find out if they had PTSD. She asked me if I would be willing to enter the program. I said, "Yes," and their testing showed that she was right. I was suffering PTSD and this program was going to give me the tools to learn to live with it. The director broke all the rules concerning my ability to stay in the House of Haole Ola' for no more than 30 days, and eventually kept me there for three months. It was there where I truly began to heal, and the "aloha spirit" was a big part of my healing. The unconditional love and most of all the safety of the place, of the island, and of the other broken women gave me the vibration of love that I needed to find the desire to return to reality. I suddenly realized that I'd lost two weeks of memory.

I reached out through the Internet to let both Andrea and Karen know where I was. I was living in the House of Hale' Ola. Karen called me one day to talk and told me that I should go to this church that she had found after researching the churches of the island on the Internet. She said, "I think you would like this one." I went to the director and asked if it would be possible for me to attend this church. She smiled and said, "That is the only church on the island that you can attend, as they pick up here every Sunday."

In my awakening from PTSD... the heart knew where I would find love. Sunday came, the van arrived, and I got in. Soon we were let out at a beautiful church. I walked in and was immediately wrapped in the arms of a three-hundred-pound island woman, who held me and hugged me like it was her mission to put my broken soul back together. It was then and there that I knew... I would return, to live life with grace and joy. Yes, I would.

Surprisingly, it was my ex-husband, Richard, who offered me that opportunity. Quite successful as a restaurateur and entrepreneur, he purchased an investment property (a luxury residence that once functioned as an assisted living facility) in Naples, Florida, and he knew that I would follow a similar path that I'd already walked before within charitable giving.

When we were married, I'd created a teen center that provided healthy activity for youth and their families, to prevent their using of alcohol and drugs. I called it Kaleidoscope—a public, nonprofit facility that not only kept kids off the streets and out of trouble, but it also provided valuable business skills for them to apply to their jobs and hobbies, for the purpose of helping them succeed in their fast-approaching adulthood. At the height of its popularity, over 200 teens came and went on weekends. Five businesses grew from that venture and kids got involved in ways that changed their lives. Still today, I hear from them on Facebook, relating the importance of that venture to the success of their lives.

There seemed to be so many people in transition who could use a roof over their heads as they worked to mend their wounds and get back on their feet, as a result of life's seemingly relentless blows. From my recent experiences, I now knew how many broken spirits there were without a place to live. So I opened "The House of Hope and Faith." My intention in doing so was to create a safe and nurturing environment—a community, really—where one could rebuild trust with loved ones, enter or re-enter the job market, gain valuable skills through education, and flourish creatively. The audience was easy, we chose addictions as once again we were fighting for the life of another son, Brian, who was living in Naples... sober, clean, and in need of support.

For whatever reason, no one in the family had realized how the death of Christopher had affected Brian, who had been there that fateful night and had waited with Chris on life support until the harvest team arrived. Between that experience and his lifelong addiction patterns, his life was slowly being eaten away.

I lived in this house along with seventeen other men and women. While it was a house that served many, it simply could not serve Brian, who soon became lost on the streets to crack, heroin, and psychotic bipolar episodes.

In spite of the challenges with Brian, my life was improving within this new life of service. Soon, I fell in love with a wonderful man and looked forward to all that this would entail, yet it didn't take long for me to realize that we would not build and share a relationship of love. All the package of history that accompanied me was more than he could handle.

While I loved Florida, I didn't like the humidity, nor was I fond of the four hurricanes that came along that year. Brian was living on the streets of Naples, in and out of jail, and I was completely unable to help him, as I now had worked the Al-anon program and learned my limits with his disease.

While I'd finally reached a point where I couldn't decide what to do with my life, fate stepped in to decide for me. Out of the blue, an investor approached me to buy the house that Richard had bought for me. From the proceeds of the sale, I was able to repay him and at long last have a nest egg that would allow me to either begin again in the world of business, or just take a few years to continue with my healing.

I called Karen and said, "I'm returning home."

She said, "I'm glad."

After a brief search, I found Brian in a rundown motel and asked him, "Do you want to return to the west coast and try and get clean?"

He said, "Yes."

While I knew it was a long shot, I couldn't leave him there.

After a little thought, I called my friend Larry Cohn. I'd met Larry at a fire walk; in fact, he was the fire walk facilitator, and we'd become very good friends. He even came to visit me when my heart had been broken by love in Florida. Larry lived in Beverly Hills, California, and had a vacation residence in Arizona that he hardly ever used. I asked him if I could live in his Arizona residence and he said, "Yes, you can live there until you decide what you're going to do."

So now armed with a plan and ready to go, I loaded up my car, picked up Brian, and drove from Florida to Arizona.

The house was like a castle, beautifully decorated, sitting in the desert in the small cowboy town of Wickenburg. I had returned with knowledge and hope for my own life and now would pick up the journey of the sisterhood of the heart with newfound enthusiasm.

Brian stayed for only a couple of days and then I put him upon a plane to go home and be with his father, as it seemed that he would be better suited there than with me.

During this quiet time, my friend Larry bought and had delivered to me a small Pekinese dog that I decided to name Precious. In all of the therapies that I have done to find peace in life, this little dog would prove to be my best medicine ever. I had her certified as a PTSD dog, and to this day she still serves me and holds my heart in a quiet place.

As my life began to move forward with a newfound sense of productivity, I began to realize the blessings I had in the friends who surrounded me and supported me in whatever way they could. A large community had grown in observing the process of the journey of the heart between Karen and I. My community became hers and she melded into my family, loving my grandchildren.

Recently, I was honored that The United States Bear Force, formed in 1982, asked me to take the role as their chair—or as we say in jest, Commander in Chief. It is a charity I have given time and love to for years. While organizations including the Red Cross and Salvation Army provide critical services and goods within hours to the sites of disasters, we focus on children, bringing them tokens of love in the form of a cuddly toy. You'd be astonished by how much that this can mean to a child during times of crisis. Currently, we also are in the process of raising funds, as well as organizing, for varied research and treatment initiatives for healing trauma-related conditions. Lord knows, that I have lived and experienced enough loss that hopefully I will be a good leader.

www.unitedstatesbearforce.org

• Twenty Five •
Whispers From Beyond the Veil

On December 2, 1967, South African heart surgeon, Christiaan Barnard and thirty members of his team performed the first human heart transplant. Louis Washkansky lived for only eighteen days, but medical science was revolutionized. I'm pausing here, bowing my head in reverence, to honor these heroes who had the courage and vision to break barriers of all kinds, and thus provide wondrous opportunities never before imagined—to me and many others.

Today, studies in the forefront of heart transplantation cite evidence of altered attitudes and behavior in recipients of hearts. Recipients have revelatory dreams that provide clues to the donor's identity, as well as either craving foods or experiencing the desire to participate in activities they didn't really care for before transplantation. This theory, called "cellular memory," proposes that the cells in our bodies contain information about our personalities, tastes, and histories, and that these characteristics can be transferred from the donor to the recipient of an organ.

The findings of Candace Pert, Ph.D., a biochemist, helped support this theory, which a growing number of scientists have now adopted. She says that, "Every cell in our bodies has its *own mind* and if you transfer tissues from one body to another, the cells from the first body will carry memories into the second body."

Dr. Andrew Amour, a pioneer in neurocardiology, suggests that the brain has two-way communication links with the "little brain in the heart." The intelligence of neural brains in organs depends on memories stored in nerve cells. Read more at: http://guardianlv.com/2013/06/organ-transplants-cellular-memory-proves-major-organs-have-self-contained-brains

Evidence of this phenomenon has been found and recorded, most prevalently in heart transplant recipients. Karen had experiences of her own and I've even witnessed these extraordinary occurrences. While some may call these events "coincidence," we believed them to be cellular memory... and as evidence of life beyond the visible.

On the first Mother's Day after Christopher's death, I was still living with Karen. She invited me out for breakfast, along with her fiancé's grandmother. It was one of her good days and she felt energetic, optimistic, and happy to be feeling well enough to celebrate with all of us, especially with her son Justin who was 15-years-old at the time.

We all got in the car, chatty and happy on an especially beautiful spring day. I hadn't asked where we were going. We pulled up to Applebee's restaurant just ahead of the Sunday church crowd, so in realizing this we quickly ran inside. Soon after taking our seats, the waitress walked over to our window seat to hand us menus. After ordering, I happened to glance outside and what I saw stunned me.

The window looked right out to the parking lot of The Big Five Sporting Goods Store, where Christopher had shot himself. Remarkably, instead of feeling grief, my heart smiled as I knew that spirit was whispering, "Happy Mother's Day, Mom."

I looked at Karen and asked, "Do you know where we are"?

She said, "I just realized".

Tears filled her eyes as she, too knew that heaven had whispered to us.

Karen later told me she'd driven to that Big Five Sporting Goods parking lot several times and just sat there, wondering where Chris had been when he'd pulled the trigger. I thought of that scene... Karen's little red Geo Tracker, matching the white one that had driven Chris to the same spot on the last day of his life. *Synchronicities.*

Karen loved Mexican food. In one of our many talks, we discovered that her most visited Taco Time Restaurant, was in Scottsdale. It happened to be the same one that Christopher used to spend hours at with his girlfriend Jessica.

Sports weren't at the top of her mind either. Karen wasn't a basketball fan until she received her new heart and then she became an avid fan of Charles Barkley and the Arizona Suns. Barkley had been Christopher's favorite player.

One of the most eventful touchstones of the heart was on Valentine's Day, 1999. My now eight-year-old granddaughter, Kristina, was visiting with me. She'd become close to Karen and wanted to take her a flower to celebrate Valentine's Day. The day before had been my birthday and Karen and I had spent the whole day together thrift shopping. We loved to go on the hunt for decorative accessories, books, and clothes at great prices. It was one our favorite hobbies to share with one another.

As Kristina asked me the question, I happened to be reflecting upon the day before. While thrift shopping I had recalled a memory. On the day Christopher had died, I had gifted him a manicure. The manicurist was my good friend. Christopher had told her of my plans to leave Ross. He mentioned that I had rented an apartment close by, and requested that she visit me more often, as he'd thought I needed a good woman friend. My friend thought this was a strange comment, as I'd had so many women friends.

There I had been, on my birthday, thrift shopping with Karen. I looked at her and realized, "I have a new woman friend and in her sits the heart of my son". Who would have known that the gift of Christopher's heart would give me that *woman friend* he thought I'd needed?

Whispers of the heart...

My mind came back into the moment and Kristina's wish to surprise Karen. I said, "Well, let's just drive by and see if she's home".

We drove to her house and knocked on her door. Her now-husband answered the door and told us that Karen and Justin had taken her computer across town to have it repaired and that they'd planned on being gone all day.

I said to Kristina, "Let's go hang out at Barnes & Noble." She loved hanging out in bookstores, so off we went. On the way, she announced that she was hungry and wanted a taco. I told her that I didn't know where we could find one in the area we were in, but asked her to watch for someplace as we drove along.

She spotted a Taco Bell, so we parked, went inside, got our tacos and sat down. I looked out the window and realized we were sitting across the street from where Christopher had run from me with the gun on the night he died.

I said to Kristina, "Honey, that's where Uncle Christopher left." She waved and said, "Hi, Uncle Chris."

She was such a spiritual child and constantly reminded me of how thin the veil is between life and death. We went on with our meal and then, Kristina said, "Grandma, look!"

I looked and there were Justin and Karen walking through the door. As soon as they saw us, they came right over to our table. Justin said, "You are not going to believe this, but mom and I have been arguing for over an hour. She needed to take her meds and wouldn't let me stop at Burger King or McDonalds. She wanted to come here and we've never been here before."

All of us knew at the same moment, that here on Valentine's Day, the day of the heart, was the appointed time of a fortuitous intersection of the hearts. We were speechless and all teary-eyed. This was truly a moment of the heart, or maybe an atonement of the heart, which actually means at-ONE-ment. Either way, it was another *whisper from beyond the veil.*

These mystical occurrences have touched upon the elemental mysteries of humankind that have been pondered throughout all of history. Are the mind and body separate from one another? The unique experiences we shared seemed to suggest that they work together as part of an interconnected system. Relatively recent research indicates that neuropeptides and their receptors are part of an underlying biological framework that assists in enabling our emotions. In search of answers to these profound questions, I sought the writings of experts in the fields of cellular memory and biomolecular medicine. Many Eastern philosophers, scientists, and physicians, as well as alternative medicine practitioners, propose that the mind and body are, indeed, one.

There seems to be a huge debate about this. On one side, you find acupuncturists, massage therapists, craniosacral practitioners, chiropractors, and hands-on-healers documenting the benefits of what's been coined "energy medicine," including famous physicians such as Deepak Chopra and Andrew Weil.

In opposition, the American Medical Association, Federal Drug Administration, insurance companies, and medical schools take a more traditional, Western approach that place the mind and body in separate domains. It is highly controversial. All sorts of studies exist to prove and disprove cellular memory, yet many recipients of major organs, especially the heart, document dreams, likes, and dislikes related to their donors.

The debate is fascinating, and goes on and on....

• Twenty Six •
A Time to Plant, A Time to Harvest

In the spring of 2008, Karen and her new husband, Bill, went to live in my ex-husband Richard's house in Beaver Creek, Oregon. Richard now had several homes across the country and was staying elsewhere. Her marriage to Russ wasn't able to survive the challenges that are often posed to a marriage due to heart transplantation. Bill, a 20 year Navy Seal, was a wondrous person that all of our healing community loved. We called him, "Mr. Bill, the keeper of the heart".

I had arranged for two of them to come to Oregon to live in this new house that had been built within a beautiful ten-acre forest. I'd also agreed to enter a business partnership with Richard and work with him in a restaurant that he was buying in Florida.

Karen derived great joy from having her hands in the earth—planting and nurturing seeds and seedlings. This was a brand new house on a Christmas tree farm that provided much room for a garden and Karen's creative vision, so I bought whatever she wanted to plant - thousands of dollars worth of plants and trees. We developed several beautiful ornamental gardens around the house, and then she planted a vegetable garden. Soon after the planting was done, Richard and I left for Florida.

In the fall of 2008, I had to fly back to Oregon. My ex son-in-law had committed suicide, taking his life on my son Brian's birthday. It was a shock to all of our family. David had a Japanese mother, and I'd loved them both dearly. (A vivid reminder that the rate of suicide is going up, not down.) I couldn't understand why he didn't contact me to share his pain, but he had, writing to an email address I no longer used. I had two more beautiful grandchildren because of him, a forever woven fabric of love.

I knew their pain. Yes, I did.

I wanted to speak at the service, so of course, I stayed in the house in the forest with Karen, surrounded by all of the beautiful evergreen trees.

One day during my visit, I saw Karen sitting in the garden harvesting all that she had planted. As I watched her, my memory trailed back to that moment in time when I heard those words, "The harvest team is here."

I looked at Karen in the middle of this big garden that she'd planted so joyously, harvesting the squash and other vegetables, and I thought *how amazing*. From that moment in time when the harvest team first showed up, I saw a link to the present; here sits the heart in the same state of the country in which it was born, harvesting vegetables. It offered me an entirely new meaning to the word "harvesting."

I also recalled the expertise of the hospital's harvest team. What intrigues me is the simultaneous process of removing one heart and replacing it with another. In preparation, they put Karen on a life support machine and took her heart out. She was technically dead. So, during the timeframe when the heart is out of the body and she's on a machine... I'm just simply curious to know where souls go when the physical body is in this state of limbo, neither dead nor alive?

Does the soul leave the body just prior to death, as many proclaim, or does it go in and out during the dying process, as stated by those having near death experiences? I wonder...

It was eight years after Christopher's death before I stopped crying every single day. We each have our way of dealing with the loss of a child. There is no road map. We each find our own way in our own time.

Once again, my life was full, joy had returned, and I was successful in business. And then the unthinkable happened. On May 25, 2009 my son Brian took his life while he was living with his father in Oregon. I had actually had a dream that his father died, and without calling anyone, got in my car in Arizona and drove to Oregon, arriving May 24.

I arrived exhausted, planning to go to their farm the next morning. The following morning I received a call from Richard that he had found Brian in a car with the motor running, he had gassed himself. My dream was not far off base, as I am sure his father feels that when he discovered Brian, he died to who he was as well.

God knows that we had tried everything to save Brian. It just seemed that Brian's broken body and mind were simply beyond worn out from his addictions. Later I found and read a 365-page manuscript that he'd written, in which he expressed how he never got over Chris' death. We were perhaps not aware enough that addicts too, can suffer grief over loss. While we were fighting the losing battle of dealing with his addictions, we somehow forgot that he had a heart that also hurt for others. I reflected back to the story Christopher had written about his dog, Grey. Was Brian the brother he talked about in the story? Just as Christopher had written in his story, Brian had driven his truck to the highest peak on the property. Had he believed as the story went... and filled his heart with love and leaped through a door into the unknown. At this point in my life, all that I knew was that there was so much more that I didn't know.

We think the unthinkable will never happen to us. How could any God expect me to lose two of my sons to suicide? It was almost unspeakable to even say out loud. I was so thankful that through the years my faith had grown stronger and that now I had it to lean upon. Had I not, I would have more than likely crumpled into despair and perhaps death, yet instead, I held onto my faith and reached out to my friends. Karen and Andrea continued to journey with me into the realm of healing. I learned the peace that passes all understanding. I held my grand children, the daughters of Brian. Together we all realized that in spite of the fact that life brings us hurricanes, typhoons, and tornadoes, that together with love we survive and we heal.

Yet again, I was writing the eulogy of a life that I'd birthed. I had brought Christopher's ashes with me on the trip to Oregon. His father and I decided to place them in the casket with Brian. I realized that I'd carried them long enough. I placed Christopher's remaining ashes into a small velvet bag, and positioned it gently under Brian's hands. I kissed Brian's forehead and thanked him for being the brother that Christopher loved.

We purchased a beautiful monument for the brothers. A place we could all go to and remember that life is eternal, and that this time here on earth is so brief. We are all aware of the suicide disease that can follow a family. I have two good friends who have also experienced the suicide of two children. Our world is harsh with the wars of the land. We must learn, be aware, and teach our little ones that there are other ways of solving problems. We must work at breaking what is becoming known as "generational suicide."

• Twenty Seven •

Identities

Karen once told me that for the longest time after the transplant, she really didn't know who she was. When I arrived in her life she was spending up to 22 hours a day on the computer; creating websites that were wholly and solely dedicated to the process. She created a beautiful site for Chris, which has since been sadly lost in cyberspace.

She said, "I had to do that because I didn't know who I was. They ripped out my heart and they gave me a new one, and not only did they give me a new one but they gave me a male heart." There is a lot of controversy around this subject, whether or not a woman should only get a female heart and a man, only a male heart.

This time when I arrived at Karen's house I brought along a copy of the video of Christopher's memorial for her to see. We were both still so numb. I didn't realize then, but years later we'd see it together once more and that the second time would be much different than the first.

When the Christmas holiday arrived in 2010, I was with Karen in her home. Some fourteen years later, she had now outlived, actually more than doubled, the original prognosis for her life span, which had been five to seven years.

She brought out the video and we sat, watching it together. It was quite something after 14 years to sit with her and watch the tape--a beautiful moment in time. Karen commented on every picture, *"Oh, look at his eyes, look at...."*

She had just noticed Christopher's curly hair, observing much more of who he was this time around. It was actually funny, almost like we were looking at it without even remembering that the heart was sitting in her chest. I wondered if enough time had gone by so that it was now truly her heart? We had gone through so much. Was it her heart? Was it my heart, our heart, his heart? We had all kinds of identities... and I thought about them all as we watched the video.

• Twenty Eight •
Walking The Fire

One day early in 1999, my friend Andrea and I were having a conversation when I suddenly made the comment, "You realize that Karen and I are like a living laboratory. How many healers do you think actually get to work with a donor mom and a heart recipient? How many have lived what Karen and I have experienced and how many would you meet who would be as willing as we are to try anything to improve Karen's life?"

Andrea gave me her quizzical Austrian look, and said, "You're right."

From that remark, she approached Jody, the owner of the Rain Star University, where she worked, asking if she could somehow integrate the two of us into a three-month project. Miracles were not new to Jody since she'd opened the school after birthing her beautiful Down's syndrome son, Joseph. Rather than allopathic treatment, she'd chosen, instead, to try alternative healing modalities. As a result of her struggles as a mother, she'd developed a wonderful and successful massage and acupuncture school.

Soon, Karen and I were part of the *Andrea Project,* a structured program that included several students who worked with us using multiple modalities, recording and documenting our experiences throughout. This was a powerful time of healing for all of us.

After we completed the term, Andrea decided to celebrate the graduation of her class with a fire walk. Fire walking is the process of burning wood down to coals and walking across the hot coals without injury. The purpose of such an activity is sometimes ceremonial and other times inspirational. Sometimes it's a combination of both. Either way, fire walking allows participants to move through their fear to the other side.

I wasn't at all interested in this and was quick to tell her, "My dear, for me just getting out of bed every day is a fire walk." I really felt it was as it seemed that I had already walked a fire that no mother ever wanted to walk. After what I'd been though over the last few years, I truly believed that I knew no fear. However, the numbness still consumed my body, and the shock still visited and settled in the marrow of my bones. Soon it was obvious to me that my dear friend, Andrea, was going to continue "holding my feet to the fire". I finally gave in and I'm glad that I did.

That firewalk was probably the most transformative thing that I had done since Christopher's death. I met the fire and overcame my fear. I met the fire, knowing that I could get burned… and *badly* too. Yet confronting this fear was a very important part of my healing.

What this fear did for me was to report to me that I was *still alive,* as most of the time, even though I put up a good front, I believed that I was the walking dead. I functioned to help the heart survive, yet not to help myself. Until that moment, I really had no other purpose, for my post-traumatic stress still owned me. As the *red alert* that lived within me, it often pulled me into its jaws of terror.

One day my phone rang. It was Dr. John Upledger. This renowned doctor, with whom Andrea had studied, ran the Institute of Craniosacral Therapy in West Palm Beach, Florida. He told me that he'd heard the "story of the heart," and said that he believed he could help both Karen and me. At the time he was working with Claire Sylvia, a heart, kidney, and double-lung recipient who had written a book entitled, *A Change of Heart,* which documented the cellular memories of the heart that she'd received. Dr. Upledger went on to say that he would waive his charges and work personally with both Karen and me if we would come to a conference in West Palm Beach, the theme of which was, *The Organs Speak.* Since the doctor believed that he could reduce Karen's need for immunosuppressant drugs, and assist me in dealing with my post-traumatic stress, it was no surprise that we said, "Yes."

By now, Karen was a willing participant in almost anything we wanted to try in the arena of alternative medicine and healing. While she had greatly benefited from her experience with Rain Star University, her health was fast failing due to the immunosuppressant drugs, which she was required to take on a daily basis. In fact, it was an astronomical amount of pills, basically a bowl full every day, and she would have to take them for the rest of her life. The drugs act like chemotherapy in that they reduce the immune system to zero so that the recipient's body won't reject the heart.

It was beyond my understanding how these drugs could actually be good for Karen's body. Her heart might not give out but I believed her body would eventually develop cancer, or one of her other organs, most likely her kidneys, would shut down from the stress.

I also encouraged Andrea to come to this conference, and see Dr. Upledger with us, since she was the catalyst for taking this project of the heart into a territory unknown. Equally important was the fact that Karen relied on and trusted Andréa's healing hands. The first time that Andrea touched Karen, her eyes filled with tears as she tried to explain what she felt in her chest. She was convinced that Christopher's heart did not settle into its cavity until the first time Andrea worked on her.

Andrea's fiancé (now her husband) generously funded this "trip of the heart." I always thought it was quite remarkable that one of the first conversations I had with Karen was to ask her if she would be willing to let Andrea come over and put her hands on her. Karen's openness to the process seemed admirable as alternative healing was a brand new territory for her.

When I witnessed Karen's health and outlook improve with Andrea's touch, I remembered how many times I'd wanted Andrea to work on Christopher. Long before he died, I knew there was more to his struggles than normal teenage crisis and had always felt that Andrea could have made a difference, but logistics always seemed to get in the way. Looking back, I wish that I'd been able to orchestrate that. Yet again, another *what if...*

Allow me a brief aside to give you a little bit of background on the very interesting Dr. John Upledger (1932-2012). He was an internationally renowned osteopathic physician who was recognized around the globe for the development of craniosacral therapy. He also ran a trailblazing education center, which offered therapeutic services, which we were about to receive for free. Although much of his life was devoted to private practice, he had also served as a highly regarded professor and clinical researcher at Michigan State University.

To give you a better idea of the importance of his work worldwide, over 100,000 practitioners, trained in more than 100 countries, have taken Dr. Upledger's classes. Many have traveled far to study with him. Needless to say, we felt honored, grateful, and excited to be working with him... his spirit and his touch were profound.

Truthfully, we were not sure if Karen would be physically up to making the trip, and by the time we arrived, she was very sick. Among everything else she'd also lost her voice, so it was a rather frightening experience overall. I prayed a lot both during and after our trip.

In spite of her illness, none of us ever wondered if we were on the wrong path because we all held the same intent, to reduce Karen's reliance on immunosuppressant drugs. Quite frankly, it was with pure determination that she made that trip.

Once we arrived at the clinic, we waited patiently for Dr. Upledger, who finally met us and chose first to work on Karen. He began the therapy by talking to her cerebellum just like it was Christopher's. He told Christopher that he could either accept this body or cause the death of another person... a very bold statement for sure. I believe in that dramatic moment, for me as a mother, the earth stood still. Something in that small room truly shifted. The earth was, for a moment, still and silent, and Dr. Upledger had seemingly reached beyond the veil.

Each day, Dr. Upledger would begin by working on us individually and then we'd go into a room filled with students, who had come from all over the world for the conference, where we would experience multi-hands-on healing. Later, looking back, I described the scene to friends as "looking like a game of *Twister*." We soon learned that as Dr. Upledger talked to Karen's body, that my body led the way.

We knew that it was the mother's body leading the heart that it had birthed and thus transcending time. The students were often in tears as they realized the magnitude of the work they were witnessing. Although I had hoped to be able to film the experience, Dr. Upledger was unwilling to allow this to happen.

Andrea, Karen, and I were soon to know that our experiences as a result of this work were sacred ones. While we were there for only a week, it took a full nine months for us to process what had happened to our bodies, minds, and spirits. Even though we couldn't really talk about it, what I do know is that as a result, Karen was able to go home and work with her doctor to significantly reduce her medications. She finally got her voice back and then began to sing again... the first time that she'd done so since receiving the heart.

I believe that somehow, as a result of both Dr. Upledger's work, and the *Andrea Project*, that at long last a connection had been created between Karen's heart and mind. While it was a long road to acceptance, it was also the beginning of my letting go.

On our last day in Florida, we went to the ocean with some of Christopher's ashes. We said a prayer and I then threw the ashes into the sea. We were stunned to watch the ashes form the exact shape of an angel on the surface of the water. Andrea ran to the car to get her camera, but by the time she returned, most of this angel image had dissipated. Yet somewhat magically, under the ashes, a giant Manta Ray (often called an *Angel Fish*) suddenly appeared. We were thrilled that we had seen this together and now continue to share this magical memory with one another.

There were many times which we experienced the "beauty" of the blessing of all of us observing a beautiful phenomena together.

• Twenty Nine •
Cellular Endings and Beginnings

It's 2013... Karen and I are both living in the beautiful mountain community of Prescott, Arizona, where we continue to see each other often. Richard bought a lovely group home and told me, once again, to do something in memory of the boys, so I opened a home for women in transition. We called this home for those coming out of drug rehab and/or prison, "The House of Life."

Bill and Karen have come to visit the ladies and me often and I also go to visit them. It's during my times at their home when we'd sit for hours discussing politics and life. Since "Mr. Bill" and I are Republicans, and Karen is a Democrat, our differences in this area of life have provided us with many lively conversations.

We continue to marvel at how far that we've all come, as well as marveling at the goodness of life. "Mr. Bill" is 20 years older than Karen and we still thought he would live forever as his larger-than-lifeness seemed to make him one who would. The many stories of his experiences around the world, serving with the Navy Seals, have filled hours on end whenever we get together.

One day, while Karen was away visiting her family in Canada, my phone rang. It was Bill telling me that he was in the emergency room and had just been told that he had pancreatic cancer. I went to the hospital to pick him up, then brought him to my house. Unfortunately, we couldn't reach Karen as she was at a lodge way up in a remote part of northern Canada. During the week that he stayed with me, Andrea and her husband Jon were also with me for the summer, so they assisted in caring for Mr. Bill as well.

I asked Mr. Bill if my home teacher could come by and give him a blessing. He said, "Yes". We all circled him and bowed our heads as the two elders gave him a blessing. Tears flowed down Mr. Bill's face as he exclaimed that, "he had seen the Christ light". Tears were streaming from everyone's faces.

As he knew death sat at his door, he continued to share how much he wanted to live so he could take care of Karen. He had taken his duty as "keeper of the heart" very seriously, and they constantly displayed the beauty of the wondrous love that they shared.

Once Karen returned, Bill decided that he would risk a surgery that ended up being a disaster from the beginning... accompanied by much pain, long nights, exhaustion, and hope suppressed as we finally realized it was only a matter of time. Eventually, we knew his time of crossing was near, and six of us gathered around his bed as we told him what his life had meant to us. I was the first to arrive at his bedside and I could see that he was very weak.

He pulled my face close and said, "I will find your boys and tell them how much you love them." Then he asked, "Will you watch over Karen?" My tears fell upon his face. How I honored this man who had loved the heart that I birthed... and he loved me too.

As I sat at his hospital bedside, holding his hand, I remembered the day in the Prescott Court House that I had stood with Karen as her maid of honor, as her son Justin gave her away to Mr. Bill in marriage. The judge loved our story and he did all that he could to make their ceremony one of sweetness. Andrea took pictures as we all celebrated a day of hearts in love and a new beginning.

On December 23, 2013, Mr. Bill quietly slipped away.

He and Karen had decided upon cremation. Karen was helpless with grief, so I pulled together a memorial, and once more, I gave the eulogy. This time, there was a twenty-one-gun salute. How ironic. This time, the sound of the gun was a sound of honor. With the final ashes of Christopher now in the coffin with Brian, I asked Karen if we could place Mr. Bill's ashes in the lovely Myrtle wood urn. Her blue eyes filled with tears as she said, "Oh, yes!"

We went together to the crematorium and gave them the urn. Soon they returned and handed the urn to her, telling her, what a beautiful piece of art that the urn was. I let the tears roll down my face as I realized what a full circle of life that we had completed. This Myrtle wood urn was now serving the remains of a man who had served our country, as well as serving the heart of Christopher. Karen and I sat there for several minutes, holding the urn and an American Flag. We could never have even imagined that coming full circle would bring us here.

Karen and I now live a life of single sisterhood, yet one that's filled with fun and adventure. We know that we have been blessed to have shared the experience of this journey with one another, and continue to witness the unfolding of life... together.

Amen.

From The Fountain of our beliefs come the graces of our lives.

The graces of my life are many...so I imagine the fountain of my

beliefs flows freely from a beautiful life-formed fountain of love.

It is the diamond-like beliefs that sparkle with life...

which flow, mingled with faith and hope.

Our beliefs are honed by experience and wisdom gained from life.

I long for non-judgment beliefs of a pure essence of love... that

allow the continuing flow of graces...

bringing peace to my life.

Caara Chantrel

Even in Darkness

We are visitors in this: that tomorrow we will reach again
for the stars and be sobered by this loss.

To strive for a higher excellence - ask more compelling questions
and work, like champions, for the discovery of an answer.

The human spirit has an uncanny capacity to endure
when it cannot find the strength to summon faith...
that this too will pass.

There is a knowing that light always follows the darkness,
and even in that darkness, there are stars in the sky.

Caara Chantrel

Epilogue

As I began to heal, I began to share my story with others and it didn't take long before I was asked to tell my story in front of various groups. The unique nature of this story seems to be one that inspires so many in any audience that I address.

However, speaking is also a continuation of my own ongoing healing process. You see, healing is not something that you do for a while, but it's something that you do every day as it's a way of life. From nearly the beginning I've found that sharing my story with others is something that's beneficial for all.

To inquire about scheduling me for a speaking engagement, simply email me at islandfirewalker@aol.com with any particulars, including city and location of event, date and time of the event, and anticipated size of audience. With all that fills my life, I require an advance notice of at least four weeks, with six to eight weeks (or more) being optimum.

In addition to scheduling me to speak for your event, Karen and I are also available to speak together, on a somewhat limited basis. Whenever we share the stage there's an unmistakable chemistry and flow between us in front of the audience that is very engaging, inspiring, and entertaining. To inquire about scheduling the two of us to speak for your event, the same contact information applies, with a minimum lead-time of ten weeks, schedules permitting.

A very early picture of Brain and Christopher, two brothers who were both lost in deaths by suicide. This is one of my favorite pictures of them together as they obviously radiate a lot of happiness.

National Suicide Prevention Hotline
1-800-273-TALK

Anyone struggling with thoughts of suicide should *immediately* dial the above number to speak with someone who can offer support.

You need not struggle with painful, dark, suicidal thoughts. It's in these thoughts that we feel alone, as though no one will understand. However, many other people have been in the exact same place and are able to offer you understanding and support.

Life has many options. Darkness and depression can be overcome. I know this is true because I have and I know that you can too.

No situation in life is permanent. Everything we experience is something that will change and more often than not, situations change for the better. We have the power to make those changes.

If dark thoughts are filling your head and the pressure of life seems to be overwhelming, *please* reach out for a helping hand.

This one life is so very precious; it's all you get.

~ *One Final Thought* ~

Sign Up for the Gift of Life at…
<u>donatelife.net</u>

In 2013 more than **47,000 corneas** were transplanted

In 2014 there were **14,414 organ donors** and **29,532 organ transplants** were performed.

As of May, 2015 there are **approximately 124,000 men, women, and children** are awaiting organ transplants in the United States alone, including 2,146 pediatric patients and 77,633 multicultural patients… all in need of the precious gift of life that can only be received through organ donation.

Each year more than 1 Million tissue transplants are completed. Each year the surgical need for tissue continues to increase.

If you have already chosen to be an organ donor, *take the time to discuss this decision with your loved ones.*

Discuss this with your family as well, especially your children when they are ready to get their drivers license.

<u>Please… make the decision that will save lives.</u>

Made in the USA
San Bernardino, CA
23 October 2016